IT'S A MAD WORLD

Travels Through a Muddled Life

Susie Kelly

blackbird

A CIP catalogue record for this book is available from the British Library
ISBN-9781838278649

© Susie Kelly 2021
Published by Blackbird Digital Books
www.blackbird-books.com
The moral right of the author has been asserted.
Cover design by First Impressions Inc
Cover Image by David Lewis, www.davidlewiscartoons.com

This is for my daughter Julie.
She has always brought me so much fun, and love. She always comes out fighting,
whatever life throws at her. I am more proud of her and love her more than I can
ever say.

'Memories warm you up from the inside.
But they also tear you apart.'
Haruki Murakami, Kafka on the Shore

Introduction

There are two basic types of people.

Those whose lives run smoothly. Their horses never sneeze and deposit green snort on their clean white shirts just as they are due to enter the ring. The heel of their shoe does not snap off on their way to an important interview. They do not arrive at work still wearing bedroom slippers. Their holidays always go exactly as planned and expected. They never lock themselves out of their own car. Their printer never breaks down without warning when it is most urgently needed. They never arrive at friends' for dinner a day early. Their cakes always rise and their dogs never jump up on the mayor covering him with mud. Neither does the mayor arrive unexpectedly when they are still wearing their pyjamas at lunchtime.

I am not one of those people. I never have been and by now I accept that I never will be. It is not that I don't try. I really do. I prepare carefully and plan ahead, but if something can go wrong, it will. It is what it is. It does make life interesting.

I have found that those people whose lives do run smoothly, even the most tolerant, tend to think it's our own fault when we stumble from one calamity to another. We must be doing something wrong. They look at us quizzically when we relate the latest disaster, as if they don't believe we can really be so inept.

This book is dedicated to those like myself, who somehow get through life and enjoy it despite whatever it throws at us.

There are some incidences of very bad behaviour. If you are likely to be outraged, you can't say you haven't been warned.

1. The Big C

I never expected to have cancer, nor did I ever expect not to have it. I never gave it any thought, but I clearly remember the moment I knew I had it.

You'll know the jokes about how to prepare for a mammogram:

Lie down on a cold garage floor and ask somebody to drive the car over your boobs until they are squashed flat. If that's not possible, find a strong person and get them to slam your boobs in the fridge door as hard as they can.

Of course, these are exaggerations. It isn't an enjoyable experience but it only lasts a few seconds and has the potential to save your life.

My mammogram reminder arrives in January. They come every two years in France, until you are 74. This is the final time I'll be invited. I add it to the pile of 'deal with this some time' papers on my desk. Each time it reaches the top, I pop it back to the bottom, because there is no urgency. In fact I may not bother this time, because I'm sure I'd know if there was anything wrong.

February and March come and go. I'm just about to screw the paper up and throw it away when I decide, no, I'll make an appointment.

Once the deed is done, and after an ultrasound scan, the radiologist calls me in to look at the results. He points out small white dots, tiny clusters of calcium. They may mean nothing, he says, but will need a further examination, which he will arrange.

Writers' antennae are finely tuned. We are alert to fleeting expressions, a change in voice tone or body language, anything that diverges from the norm (because we may want to use it in our writing).

Handing me my X-rays, the radiologist takes my hand in both of his and says he hopes everything will be OK. That's when I know, because usually – I've been seeing him every two years for a decade – he just shakes my hand and wishes me *bonne journée*. This time he is sending a message.

I decide not to worry, and not to mention anything to anybody until I know more.

Three weeks later, I'm having a stereotactic biopsy procedure, lying face down on a hospital table with a hole in it through which the suspect boob is inserted. The table is high enough from the floor to enable the technicians below to do their job, which is to precisely locate the suspect cells and remove them for examination.

It's painless, done under local anaesthetic and takes about half an hour. I suppress a small giggle, thinking this is how a cow must feel during milking. The nurses and doctor treat me as gently as if I were made of spun sugar. One nurse talks to me, occasionally patting me on the back and asking if I am OK. I mention that my neck is uncomfortable after lying on my front for 15 minutes, so she massages it until the procedure is finished, then she wraps me in a warmed blanket.

It will take a couple of weeks before I have the results confirmed, so in preparation for treatment that I know will make my hair fall out, I start looking for headwear, and am pleasantly surprised to see what a wide selection there is to choose from. There are colourful turbans and glamorous jewelled beanies, silky scarves and cute little cotton hats with faux fringes. I select a couple to order when the time comes.

It's been five weeks since the mammogram, and today I'm back at the hospital for the results of the biopsy.

When I go into the breast doctor's office, the first thing she says is: 'Have you come alone?' The antennae twitch. That's a very strong signal. When I reply that I have, she glances at the intern who is there with her, and I read the silent signal in her eyes. Twitch, twitch.

Their discomfort is tangible; they don't want to be doing this and I want to say to them: 'It's OK, you can tell me. I am not afraid. I am ready.'

The doctor asks whether I understood the purpose of the stereotactic biopsy, and I reply that I do.

So, she says, it shows two tumours, each of two centimetres, and they are cancerous. She is looking right into my eyes as she says it. The intern is also watching me intently. I feel I should be doing something theatrical. They are expecting me to scream, or faint, throw a fit of hysterics or burst into tears, but I am completely, absolutely calm and simply nod.

She continues gently. 'It means a total mastectomy, which I will perform. There will be no further treatment necessary because the tumours are contained. They have not spread.'

Inappropriately, I feel a fleeting disappointment that I won't need to buy the pretty headwear.

She goes on. 'At the same time you will have reconstructive surgery.'

She explains there are three options: a silicone implant, tissue from my stomach, or a muscle from my back. I can go home and think about it, or decide straight away, which I do. I go for the back muscle option.

She says: 'I'll see if the plastic surgeon is free.'

She makes a phone call, and a few minutes later the door opens. In walks the plastic surgeon, straight out of a Mills and Boon novel, or a television medical drama. He's young and extremely handsome, with long lashed brown eyes and a generous, kind smile. Beneath his white coat he's wearing jeans and trainers.

He asks politely if I will remove my top so he can have a look, and then he asks what cup (*bonnet* is the French word) size I'd like.

I look at him blankly. I'm stuck for words. It's all happening so quickly.

'Um, smaller.' I say.

'How about a 'B' cup?' he suggests.

'Yes, that would be perfect.'

'OK.' he says, shaking my hand. 'No problem.'

While I put my clothes back on, he and the breast doctor synchronise their diaries and set a date for the operation.

'Don't worry,' the doctor reassures me, 'there is no urgency. The tumours are in situ, and they have not spread. And you'll have a wonderful view of Poitiers from your room on the ninth floor.' she smiles.

She couldn't have said anything more alarming. My heart thuds and I feel a red flush of panic. There's the ground floor, then floor 0 where the operating theatres are and then the technical floor before you even reach floor No. 1 which is actually four floors and 66 steps up, so technically the ninth floor is 13 floors up, and I am extremely claustrophobic. I always walk up the stairs to the first floor, arriving wobbly-kneed and breathless, but there is no way I can climb 13 flights of stairs.

'But, I'm claustrophobic, I can't go in a lift!' I squeak. She looks at me in silent astonishment, as if she cannot understand anybody who finds the prospect of having to get in a lift a million times worse than facing a mastectomy.

In the last half hour, I have had the most other-worldly experience of my life.

*****

Driving home, my only worry, aside from the lift, is telling my daughter. Some years ago, she lost her dearest friend as a result of breast cancer, and I know that my news will cause her immense anxiety. I decide not to mention anything about it to anybody until the day before the operation, except to my husband Terry, who is understandably shocked, and my lovely editor and publisher Stephanie because I planned to deliver a new manuscript this year, and I'm not sure I'll be able to do so.

Having always been squeamish, I'm surprised that I spend several hours watching videos to see exactly how the *latissimus dorsi* procedure is performed, and am left in awe of modern medicine. With my curiosity satisfied, for the next couple of months I put it out of my mind.

A week before the operation, I need to have another mammogram. The radiologist asks if I am anxious about having the operation. I say that I'm not, I have total faith in the French health service. He asks about the reconstruction, and I tell him that I will be having a reduction.

5

His eyes shoot open and his face is a picture of dismay. 'A REDUCTION? Why?'

'Because,' I reply, 'I want them to be smaller. They are too big.'

He takes my hand, and says slowly and very clearly: 'Madame, they are NEVER too big.' I leave there laughing.

On the morning of the operation, I arrive at the hospital and face my worst fear: the steel lifts. There are six of them, and a touch pad where you select the floor you are going to, and it tells you which lift to take. My mouth is dry and I'm on the verge of tears, but there's bugger all I can do except step inside. Terry squeezes my hand, and sooner than I would have thought possible the automatic lady announces 'Ninth floor' and the doors open. The worst is over.

My room is bright and, as the doctor promised, gives a fine view over the city. Various people come in with files and clipboards and papers to sign, and I put on the ghastly shapeless gown that is made for a giant and difficult to do up at the back.

The breast doctor comes to have a brief chat and assure me that everything will be fine, of which I have do doubt at all. She is followed by the plastic surgeon, with his smile and gentle eyes. He undoes the gown at the neck and carefully wraps it around my waist to preserve my modesty. Then he takes a blue felt-tip pen from his breast pocket and begins drawing lines all over my chest and back. I look down at his head, thinking what lovely hair he has and wonder what he'd do if I stroke it.

With my chest decorated like a pentacle as if in preparation for a satanic ritual, I climb back into bed and wait.

When I have had operations previously, a nurse would come with a sedative to take an hour before you went to theatre, but they don't seem to do that any more, or maybe they only do if you seem agitated. I read on my Kindle until the porters come to wheel me away. The bed rumbles down the corridor, which is narrow so that personnel have to flatten themselves against the wall as we pass, around a corner and halting at the lift door. It's a very narrow lift, with only room for the bed with the two porters. I gulp and listen to them complaining about somebody who has done something to upset them both. Before I can find out more, the doors open and we're off again, at racing speed, along more corridors and into a pre-operating waiting room.

There's a TV on the wall, several other patients are waiting on their beds to go into theatre. The nurses chat cheerfully as they move stacks of towels and gowns in and out of cupboards, deal with patients and answer phone calls. My anaesthetist introduces herself and asks if I have any questions, then inserts a needle into the back of my hand, where the anaesthetic will go, and says she'll see me later in theatre.

I watch the TV for a while, until I'm wheeled out into the corridor and moored alongside a very narrow bed which I have to shuffle onto. It isn't easy when you are lying on your back and trying to keep the frightful gown from exposing your rear, but after an undignified struggle I'm aboard, covered with a warm blanket and wheeled into the cool theatre beneath a cluster of bright lights.

With a great number of people moving around, talking and laughing, it feels like a cocktail party.

From childhood stays in hospital, I remember nurses scrub-faced, cool, brisk, detached, with their hair brutally confined beneath starched caps. Unapproachable, to be obeyed without question. Tugging and smoothing bedsheets tightly before Matron's terrifying round. I recall feeling slightly afraid of them, anxious not to do anything wrong in the perpetual silence that was only broken by the tinkle of a thermometer and rustle of a crisp uniform.

Poitiers is a university hospital, and the majority of the staff are young. Under their white coats they wear casual clothes and shoes; some have tattoos and visible piercings. The girls have their hair loose and wear make-up, jewellery and colourful uniforms. They chatter merrily with each other and with patients. They are professional, and also fun, making you feel like a person, not just a patient. I find it much less intimidating.

The anaesthetist smiles down at me and places a mask over my face. Breathe deeply, she says. It's just oxygen.

I breathe as deeply as I can for a minute, and she asks if I am starting to see the room moving or fading out. I shake my head. 'Keep breathing', she says, 'I'm going to start putting you to sleep now.' I keep breathing, and the room is still as clear as a clear thing.

*****

Seven hours later, I'm back in bed in my room, wide awake and hungry. There's a drip in my arm and I can feel dressings around my chest, but no pain at all.

I sleep through the night and wake up feeling absolutely bright and cheerful, able to sit up and walk to the bathroom.

Nurses are in and out, taking my blood pressure and temperature, checking dressings and asking what I would like for lunch from a wide choice including several vegetarian options. Terry and a friend come to visit, and both look taken aback to see I'm sitting up and looking perfectly well and normal. I don't feel any different to how I felt the previous day.

After my evening meal, I read for a little before dropping off into a deep sleep. I'm awakened some time during the night by the beautiful plastic surgeon leaning down and saying they are taking me back to '*le bloc*', which is what the operating theatre is called in France. I have developed a very large haematoma and he will have to operate again. I don't remember what happened next, but when I awoke next morning, there were three drains inserted in my back to remove accumulated fluid. Wherever I go, I must wheel the drip and tow the drains around like plastic puppies, making sure not to trip over their leads. Every two hours they are checked, it seems the bleeding will never stop and I'll be emptied dry. I try using all my mental force to stop the bleeding, which seems to work because eventually the puppies are empty and I'm discharged nine days later.

For a few days after, I am home and feeling fine. Each morning, one of our wonderful local nurses comes to change the dressings. When I start feeling slightly unwell, I put it down to the reaction of having two general anaesthetics within two days, and the various medications I am taking, but when the nurse arrives she takes one look and sends me immediately back to hospital. Going down the stairs, I miss my footing and slither down on my back, but happily Terry catches me before I go too far.

Back in hospital, enveloped in the awful gown, lying on the speeding trolley, into the lift and down into the pre-operating room, once again writhing inelegantly from my bed onto the operating table, the needle is in my hand, the mask on my face, I drift pleasantly away.

I wake up to the news that the surgeon has removed a large, deep-seated abscess from what is, by now, my rather battered and considerably smaller left boob.

Now I develop a resistant infection. It's high summer and the temperature bounds into the low 40s. With no air conditioning on the ninth floor, the poor nurses, who are somehow managing to function in the stifling conditions, place iced flannels on our heads and tuck freezer packs around our bodies. Terry arrives with a huge fan that stirs the sticky air bringing slight relief.

The infection persists. I have a blood transfusion. Watching the blood travel from the transparent bag and through the tube into my veins, I idly wonder who it had previously belonged to. My own blood is sent to a centre for tropical diseases to see whether they can find something to kill whatever it is that is preventing me from healing.

Another new drug, another five days, then finally the infection is beaten and I can go home. During the next year, I'll have two more surgeries to repair the damage caused by the abscess, and to make both appurtenances the same size.

All surgery carries the risk of haematomas and/or infections. Some people don't experience either; I have managed to have both, but even with these complications, my overall experience has been neither frightening nor painful. I know that I have been extremely lucky, luckier than those who have had to undergo long-term and drastic treatments. Sometimes I wonder how things would have turned out if I hadn't decided to have that mammogram when I did, and I hope that any ladies reading this will be encouraged and reassured.

Why I have not been in the least anxious throughout the whole affair I can't really explain, but possibly it's because I'm a pragmatist, and as a writer I have been intensely fascinated with everything that is happening around me.

*****

I'm under orders to take life easy. Terry brings me breakfast in bed every day. He has even learned to cook (I would never have imagined that was possible!). Before my diagnosis, we had discussed where we would go for our next holiday this year – maybe Warsaw, possibly Istanbul or somewhere in Albania. Now we accept we won't be going anywhere, because I tire easily and have follow up hospital appointments every couple of weeks.

Travel is oxygen to me. Although I'm pampered and can enjoy the peace of our garden, I still yearn for the thrill of planning a visit to somewhere new, the excitement of booking tickets and accommodation; sometimes I become tearful realising that for this year it isn't going to be possible.

I search for an antidote to this melancholy, to stop feeling sorry for myself and be grateful for what I have.

First of all, I re-read all the previous books I've written, to remind myself I've had a pretty good and interesting life so far. Then I start going through my old diaries and photo albums.

As the lovely Simon Reeve writes in his autobiography *Step by Step*, 'it is always worth remembering that some of the most memorable times can happen when things go a bit wrong'.

Of all the many places we have been and the things we had done, those that remain most vivid in my memory are mostly when things didn't go quite, or even at all, how I hoped or expected. Even if at the time they were frightening or frustrating, looking back they are the ones that still make me smile, or sometimes feel mildly surprised to have survived.

We have spent many holidays in luxury hotels around the world where the weather was fine, the food was delicious, the room had a splendid view. Apart from having the bed made and the bathroom cleaned every day, there is not much that appeals to me. Shiny floors, flower arrangements, obliging staff. It was nice. None of it makes any lasting impression and a couple of weeks after we've left, I have virtually no memory of what it was like. Great for chilling out and recharging the batteries but not memorable. I prefer going to places where each day is unpredictable, and preferably where I can learn something.

As the months of convalescence segued into Covid lockdown and the prospect of travel seemed ever further away, I retained my sanity by reliving and enjoying some of my most memorable moments as I've muddled along through life.

Here they are. I hope you enjoy them too.

2. The Muddy Child

It's the mid-1970s. After the drama of recovering my children from my ex-husband (*I Wish I Could Say I Was Sorry*), life starts to move forward and settle into a comfortable rhythm. I'm a single mother with two young children and we're doing pretty well. Money is tight but I'm scraping by, until my car breaks down at work and I can't afford to call out a garage.

One of my colleagues finds the fault and fixes it temporarily, offering to come at the weekend to replace the defective part. I accept gratefully, and invite him to join us for lunch to thank him.

We sit down to eat, when Julie, who is six, asks in a loud voice: 'Is he going to be our new dad?'

I squirm with embarrassment, and he raises an eyebrow in my direction.

'Shall we take the kiddies out this afternoon?' he asks.

I plead a visit from friends. It will take many weeks for him to accept that he is not going to be our new dad. I do not want a new dad in the family and am happy with the status quo after all the trauma of the previous couple of years.

A couple of months later, Terry, who had helped me when I returned from Kenya with the children, calls around for coffee one day. He asks if we'd like to go sailing on a nearby lake. He hires a dinghy and gives us our first sailing lesson. Julie is quick to understand the principle.

'Is the secret not to fall in?' she asks.

The following weekend, Terry invites us all to spend a day out on the East coast. I'm pleased at the prospect of an outing somewhere new, and the children are excited. I visualise us on a sandy beach frolicking in the sunshine and enjoying the sea air.

We've been driving for half an hour when Julie announces she is going to be sick. Terry pulls the car over and we lift Julie out onto the grass verge, where she vomits copiously. I'm very bad with vomit and have to fight not to come out in sympathy, but Terry holds her until she's empty and wipes her face clean.

The blackcurrant juice she drank before we left has all come out and her clothes are stained in an abstract pattern of purple streaks

When we arrive at our destination, I take her to a children's clothing shop and buy her a nice set of pink dungarees and a little pink jumper, consigning her purple-streaked clothes to the boot of the car.

It's a mild, sunny day, and we walk down a jetty towards the sea. The tide is far out. Holding her hand, I jump down onto the beach. We land in deep, squishy mud which looked on the surface to be dry and firm. It's halfway up my legs, and almost up to the waist of Julie's new pink dungarees.

When I pull her out and up back onto the jetty, she asks: 'Mummy, why did you push me into the mud?'

Terry has friends in the town, and so we go and knock on their door. A delightful lady invites us in, puts the kettle on, runs a bath, puts Julie into it, washes her dungarees and underclothes, pops them in the drier, and rinses the mud off her shoes.

Fortified with coffee, cake and two clean children, we find a family-friendly pub for lunch. An elderly waitress asks the children if they are having a nice day and says what a lovely family we are. Pointing at Terry, Julie explains: 'He's not our real dad.'

On the drive back, she vomits once again, so I arrive home with two bags of wet and malodorous clothing to wash.

I doubt we'll be invited again.

3. The Jolly

Much to my surprise after our trip to the East coast, Terry invites me to go sailing at Easter with his friends who own an ocean racing yacht.

If I'm honest, the sea has never held much attraction for me. I'm an Aries, a fire sign, and I nearly drowned once. I'll tell you about it later. Like many other things, I am actually quite afraid of the sea.

As a very small child, I spent our annual family holidays at Bournemouth, with its beautiful sandy beach and intriguing rock pools. I was never keen to go in the water because of the slimy seaweed that wrapped itself around my ankles like a clump of serpents, but I was happy enough sitting building sandcastles with my bucket and spade. I never had any frightening experiences there, so it will always be a mystery where the terrifying dream came from.

It started when I was six and recurred at least half a dozen times over the next few years.

I dreamed I was alone on the beach. The sky was a clear blue, and the calm sea was gently lapping at the sands. Behind me was a tall cliff. As I watched the surf tickling my toes, the sea began to slowly recede, leaving an expanse of golden sand reaching to the horizon. The sea vanished completely. I stared out over the sand to where a dark line appeared in the far distance. It slowly grew up towards the sky, until I could see it was a giant wave, curling upwards and coming towards the beach. While I stood there, it grew higher and higher until it was directly above me, then began to curl overhead, so I was standing in a translucent green tunnel. With the cliff behind me there was no way to escape and I knew the wave would trap me beneath it as it collapsed.

I would wake from the dream with my heart pounding.

In 2004, the news reported the devastating tsunami in the Indian

Ocean. Watching the horror of it on the television brought back that dream that had haunted me almost fifty years before. The dream of a tsunami, something I had never seen or heard of and yet had dreamed of with such clarity.

When, as a child, I first sailed to our new life in Kenya I loved life aboard the ship, but I didn't like looking at the vastness of the sea, with its terrible unknown depths. On my first honeymoon, we sailed from Mombasa to Cape Town around the Cape of Good Hope where the Atlantic and Indian oceans meet, and I saw the full might of the seas. While the liner was tossed from side to side and front to back for days on end, passengers were confined to their cabins except for mealtimes. We had to cling to ropes strung along the passageways as we battled our way to the dining room, tilting from side to side. A huge wave caused the band to be thrown from the stage and slither across the dance floor, drums and cymbals rumbling and clattering. Tarpaulins were strapped from upper to lower decks to prevent people from being washed away if they were unhinged enough to try to walk on the decks. We had to sleep on the cabin floor to avoid being tossed off the beds. During mealtimes there was a constant noise of crockery being smashed as the ship hurtled up and down. Stewards poured water over the tablecloths to prevent the plates and cutlery from slipping off. One particularly violent lurch tipped the people sitting opposite us backwards off their chairs so they slid the width of the dining room with their legs in the air, before bumping into the furthest table. I was horrified at the power of the ocean that could toss 15,000 tons of ship about like a cardboard box. It's too strong, too deep, merciless.

Still, the idea of lounging on the deck in a bikini, sipping a dry Martini with an olive, like the girl on the television ad, has its appeal, so I accept the invitation. I go and buy a new bikini in dark blue with gold trimmings. Terry's mother is happy to look after the children for the day.

'We won't actually be racing,' explains Terry. The season hasn't begun yet so today will be what they call a 'jolly' – sailing around locally for the crew to get the feel of the new boat. Just a bit of fun.

It's a shame that when the day arrives, the weather has deteriorated and the bikini won't be needed. Instead, I'm wearing jeans, a jumper and a lightweight jacket.

The owner of the 30-foot boat is a large, hearty man who gives me a big hug and says I should go below (I mustn't refer to it as 'downstairs') and put the kettle on. I'm shocked by how primitive the boat is. The narrow deck is cluttered with winches and ropes. The cockpit is filled with a huge steering wheel; the downstairs space just holds canvas bunk beds, a heap of canvas bags containing sails, a tiny swinging gas hob, a teeny sink and a little fridge containing a bottle of milk and some mouldy breadcrumbs. Nothing at all like the cosy cabin with comfortable chairs and panoramic windows that I was expecting.

I find some teabags and mugs and boil the kettle. When I pour the milk into the first cup, it rockets to the surface in lumps.

'Do you have any fresh milk?' I call up to the deck. 'This bottle is off.'

Somebody shouts down that it doesn't matter, as long as it's hot and sweet, so I tip a load of sugar into each mug and hand them up.

I can hear more people coming aboard, running up and down the deck, shouting and laughing. I make more cups of tea and clean out the fridge with a damp cloth hanging on the edge of the sink.

After a while the boat starts to move, inch by inch. Looking up through the hole in the roof (hatch), I see yellow rubber boots moving around. I wonder if it will be OK to close the door over the hatch because it is very cold down here.

I stick my head out and try to attract attention, but everybody is busy winding winches and humping sail bags about, so I draw my head back in, like a tortoise, and sit rubbing my arms up and down, wondering how long jollies last.

Although there is almost no sense of movement as I know it, I can hear the men congratulating each other at getting the boat speeding along.

Time passes as I get colder and colder, and start to feel very tired. I've stopped shivering and am sitting staring at my knees when Terry comes down to see if I'm enjoying myself. As soon as he sees me, he realises that I'm not; not at all. I'm starting to suffer from hypothermia. He rummages around in some cupboards (lockers is what they are called) beside the bunks, and pulls out a couple of thick sleeping bags that smell of damp and feet. He wraps them around me and finds a woolly hat that he sticks on my head, then rubs my arms and legs briskly. He makes me a cup of hot water as there are no teabags left.

I gradually defrost and come around. When I peer outside through the hatch, I see that it's snowing hard. There's a lot of movement on the deck. The sails are coming down, and the engine is switched on. Half an hour later, we are back on land, where it is still snowing hard. I can't remember ever being so cold, and I hope I won't be invited again. Jolly this event wasn't. Without wanting to sound ungrateful, that was the most ghastly afternoon I can remember for many years.

4. The Silly Bitch

Three months later, I'm back again on the boat. Summer has arrived and the weather is pleasant. From previous experience, I know I won't be needing the bikini as there is no deck space on which to lounge. Instead, I'll sit in the cockpit and read, although Terry is rather irritated when I mention it, because he says I am there to enjoy the sailing, not to sit with my nose in a book.

This time it's a club event, a race on the river Crouch in Essex.

The boat's owner welcomes us aboard with a glass of bubbly. He calls me 'my lovely' and 'sweetheart', and his wife hands around a tray of smoked salmon sandwiches. She is going to entertain my children with her own while we are sailing. This will be the boat's first real test of speed. The crew stand around discussing tactics while I sip the bubbly and munch on the sandwiches.

As the boat motors from its mooring and out onto the river where a dozen other similar boats are milling around, I stand on the deck with my sandwiches and glass of fizz, feeling sporty and sophisticated.

The engine is switched off, the crew are winding winches and uncoiling ropes (they are called sheets), and I'm watching to see what will happen next, when a gun goes off and the boat's owner yells:

'Get that silly bitch out of the way!'

I look around for the silly bitch, and realise it is me.

Terry calls: 'Get down below,' so I scramble out of the cockpit, climb through the hatch and sit on a bunk. I pull out my book and read for a while.

I call out to ask if I should be making tea. Nobody answers, so I go back to the book.

There's a lot of shouting, feet pounding on the deck, and I can hear the winches clacking. An arm reaches through a hole in the roof at the front of the cabin (there's probably a technical term for that but I don't know it) and hauls up one of the canvas sail bags.

The language is as foreign to me as Japanese, and every shout carries an implicit exclamation mark.

'Ready about!'

'Jibe!'

'Water!'

'Lee oh!'

Swear words, too.

Peering out of the hatch I see we are surrounded by other boats, their crews scurrying about the decks as sails go up and down. The sails have their own sail bags and their own names: spinnaker, blooper, jib, genoa – rather like Santa's reindeer.

The boats don't go in a straight line like greyhounds or racehorses. Instead they zigzag from side to side, (tacking) to catch the wind in their sails. It looks pretty chaotic and I won't be at all surprised if they bump into each other.

Also, unlike greyhounds and racehorses, as far as I can see the fleet is barely making any forward progress, although from the deck a voice whoops that we are 'pissing along'. Later I learn that we reached eight knots, slightly over nine miles an hour. Apparently that's fast for these yachts.

After two hours, we cross an invisible line in the water and a gunshot signals that we have won. There's much cheering and backslapping and I am upgraded back to 'My lovely' and allowed upstairs.

5. The Witch

Ocean racing is Terry's passion. Not a hobby or a pastime, but a full-blown passion. His diary for the year reveals that every summer weekend he is going to be racing. I won't be going; there's no room for passengers on a racing yacht. In any case, I don't have a competitive cell in my body and would be useless even if I knew how to sail.

The 40-foot yacht he is navigating is campaigning for selection in the British Admiral's Cup team. It's the premier event in the ocean racing calendar, held every two years during Cowes Week on the Isle of Wight.

On a cross-Channel race to Le Havre, one of the crew is swept overboard by the boom (long thing that supports the bottom of the sails and swings from side to side). He cannot swim and is not wearing a safety line or a flotation jacket. Although the crew slash the sails to bring the boat to a halt and throw him life jackets as he flails in the water, he sinks out of sight and is lost forever.

Strangely, when his mother is told of his death, she is not surprised. She says she already knew: his dog began to howl at the same time as her son fell overboard.

The boat's owner withdraws from the campaign. Terry is highly regarded as a navigator, having previously navigated one of the winning British Admiral's Cup teams. He is quickly snapped up by the Italian team on one of their 45-foot boats.

He reports that life aboard is punctuated by frequent noisy fights between crew members arguing about tactics and carelessly ripping the expensive sails. He says they stand little chance of winning any races, as they stop racing at mid-day to enjoy leisurely lunches on the deck. Still, the food and wine are excellent and the crew are charming and fun, and at least he will be sailing.

The Italian team takes over an exclusive hotel on the Isle of Wight for Cowes Week, and Terry extracts an invitation for me to accompany him there.

The owner of the boat is a gracious, serious man married to the heiress of an oil fortune. She is slim, blonde, perfectly tanned and bursting with the self-confidence that only being a billion-heiress can bring. When Terry introduces me to her she totally ignores me, turning away to speak to someone else. If it wasn't for the fact that I'm her guest and beholden to her for the beautiful room we are staying in, the exquisite food served at every meal and the fleet of hired Alfa Romeo cars that take us to and from the hotel to the harbour every day, I'd think she was rather rude.

Happily the weather is as perfect as an English summer can be when it's at its very best, almost as if it has been bought with the oil money. During the day, the crew are sailing the boat while I'm free to entertain myself, which I do, sunbathing in the grounds of the hotel, reading, and walking around the flowery country lanes. Sometimes I go with the crew to the harbour and enjoy the merriment of the regatta, eat ice cream and sip Pimms, watching the boats sailing in the sunshine. I don't go every day because on the second morning while we are standing around waiting for the cars, the heiress says in Italian in a loud voice to her journalist friend, a woman who dresses like a man: 'Get in quickly when the car comes. We don't want *quella la* with us.' I was referred to as *quella la* in a previous life. It means 'that one'.

I don't bear her any malice. I've been thrust upon her and am enjoying her reluctant hospitality, so she doesn't owe me anything. The following days I hang back until all the cars are full, unless somebody invites me in.

Her husband is terrified of being kidnapped, or having their young son kidnapped. At home in Italy he is chauffeur-driven in a bullet-proof car, delivered door-to-door wherever he's going, and permanently accompanied by armed bodyguards.

Two of his bodyguards are crewing on the boat. They both carry guns.

One of them, Franco, whom we call Frank the Rod, suggests to Terry that they should kidnap the boss, collect a massive ransom – 'His wife can afford it,' laughs Frank – and retire to a tropical island.

I'm sitting next to Frank the Rod at dinner the first evening, enjoying a glorious five-course meal. He shows me a photograph of his wife.

'She don't come,' he says. 'That one,' he nods at the billion-heiress, 'is bitch. Hate all woomin. Want all man for her. Nobody bring they woomin here. Look – you see no woomin.' He gestures around the dining room. Apart from the Italian female journalist who dresses like a man and seems to be the wife's very close friend, I am the only other female present.

'No worry, Susie,' says Frank the Rod. 'No take any notice *La Strega* (The Witch). You very beautiful. Put hand down here.' He takes my hand and directs it to his lap, which is sporting a healthy erection. 'If I want you, I take you.' he continues.

I burst out laughing, and he joins in.

'Be 'appy, always be 'appy,' he says.

After dinner we all move into the hotel's lounge, a gracious room filled with plump armchairs and sofas. There's a log fire burning, although the night is warm. Everybody is sitting around talking about sailing, except for one handsome, solitary man wearing slacks and a grey cardigan, who is standing on his own gazing around the room and looking a little lost. Sensing a kindred spirit, I go over to him and ask whether he's crewing on one of the boats.

'No,' he says. 'I am a guest. What about you?'

I say I am also a guest, a non-sailing one.

'What is your name?' he asks.

'I'm Susie.'

He bows slightly and holds out his hand.

'Gianni Agnelli.'

Across the room I catch the icy glare of *La Strega* as she breaks away from her group of admirers, strides towards us and leads away one of Italy's richest and most influential men. *Ciao* Gianni.

Once more alone, I go out onto the verandah for a while and then go to visit the ladies' room.

When I come back I can't see anybody else on their own, so I stand in front of the fire and watch the logs flickering.

I am suddenly aware of hands stroking my ankles. *Why would anybody be doing that?* They slowly move up to my knees.

I wonder if it's a joke at my expense. Is it *La Strega's* idea? Somebody is to run their hands up my legs, so that I will turn around angrily, and shout, maybe slap a face, to the amusement of the spectators. They continue their conversation as if nothing is happening, waiting for the moment when I snap, whereupon they will all cheer and laugh.

Deciding not to give them that satisfaction, I keep gazing resolutely into the fire while the hands move up above my knees. As they continue their ascent, I turn my head slightly, and look down into the upturned face of Frank the Rod crouching behind me.

'What are you doing, Frank?' I ask, trying to sound like a good sport but also slightly shocked.

'You dress is tuck in you panties. I try to take it out for you.'

*****

The week has passed quickly, it has been a lot of fun, and on the final evening we enjoy a gala banquet before retiring to the drawing room, where *La Strega* is holding court, with all the men standing around her in an obedient circle.

Once, long ago, at a company function in a restaurant we were all throwing bread rolls at each other, and for some reason I picked up an empty wine bottle and threw it at one of the guests. It seemed to have left my hand as if it had taken on a life of its own, because throwing bottles at people is not something I had ever done before, nor since. Luckily, it bounced harmlessly off a window frame and no damage was done, but it was the strangest thing, because in my right mind I would never do anything like that. I wasn't drunk, there was no explanation; it felt as if I was being operated by remote control.

Now something similar happens, the robot is operating again and I find myself squeezing through the circle of men and walking up to *La Strega*, who stops in mid-speech with her mouth half-open.

I smile at her, and say, in Italian, that I want to thank her for her generosity, how much I appreciate being invited, how pleased I am that her husband's boat has done so well, and what a lovely little boy she has. For a moment she is paralysed with shock, but she recovers quickly and replies: 'Oh, I didn't know you spoke Italian.'

'I only speak a little,' I reply sweetly. 'But I understand most things.'

I can see her recalling all the unpleasant comments she has made about me in my earshot. Over her shoulder, Frank the Rod has a huge smile on his face. He winks.

Tossing her beautiful blonde mane, she murmurs: '*Molto bene,*' waves her hands at the admirers like somebody shooing geese, and the circle breaks up.

As Frank the Rod passes, he whispers '*Brava, bella.*'

6. Broken

Two years later. It's the summer of 1979 and we're back at Cowes. Once again the weather is perfect, with clear blue skies and warm sunshine. This time Terry is navigating on an English-owned 45-foot racing yacht, and we're spending a few days jollying around the Solent before the start of the Fastnet Race.

Yesterday, there was a strong wind driving powerful waves. I was allowed up on deck where we all had to keep scrambling from one side to the other to sit with our feet dangling over the side as the boat changed tack, ducking under the swinging boom so as not to be knocked off. For the first time, I understood the lure and exhilaration of ocean racing to the men, wrestling the wind and water as the boat is smacked and bounced up and down onto the waves.

The following day, we are out for a final sail before I return home ahead of the 600-mile race from Cowes to the Fastnet Rock on the southern tip of Ireland, finishing at Portsmouth. Today, the crew are tuning the boat and I'm directed to sit below and read.

When I look up from my book after half an hour, I notice a shallow puddle of water around my feet which I am fairly sure was not there earlier. I put my head up through the hatch and call up to the nearest pair of boots: 'There's water down here.'

The boots reply: 'Don't worry darling. It's a boat – they get wet!'

I retreat to my book. Over the next hour, the water around my feet has been rising noticeably and is now a couple of inches deep, but I don't want to be a wimp or a nuisance, so I keep reading. Through the hatch I can hear a lot of frantic shouting.

When the water is over four inches deep so that I have to sit with my feet up on the bunk to avoid them getting wet, I yell up to Terry. He comes over to the hatch and says irritably: 'What? You have to entertain yourself. We've got a problem. Somebody is going to have to get in the water and see if we've picked up something on the prop. We can't get any speed. We're almost going backwards.'

'I'm sorry,' I say, feeling totally unreasonable and also in some inexplicable way as if I'm responsible for the water getting in and the boat almost going backwards. 'But there does seem to be a lot of water down here and it's getting deeper all the time.'

He pushes his head through the hatch and says a rude word, then starts to shout. Another head appears, and another, and on the deck everybody is shouting and rushing around. The boat is leaking. Down come the sails and we motor quickly back to the harbour.

Inspection reveals a crack in the hull, certainly caused by the violent slapping up and down yesterday. The boat will not be taking part in the Fastnet Race. While everybody is disappointed, they're thankful the damage has been discovered close to home, and not in mid-race, offshore.

We've been home two days, then on the third day of the Fastnet Race the news begins to come in of a sudden, destructive storm raging at Force 10 in the Irish Sea. Boats are capsizing, sustaining severe damage as their masts are snapped off and their sails reduced to rags. They are tossing uncontrollably on mountainous waves. Crews are having to abandon and take to the sea, relying on lifeboats, helicopters, navy and merchant vessels to rescue them.

Twenty hours later the storm is still wreaking havoc.

My office phone rings constantly, with friends calling to ask hesitantly if there is any news of Terry. Thanks to that cracked hull I am able to reassure them that he is safe on dry land.

By the end of the race, many boats have been destroyed, very few managing to complete the race. Fifteen sailors have lost their lives.

*****

The thing about ocean racing is that there is no room for passengers. The boats are stripped out to be as light as possible and every member of crew has to function efficiently. Competition to be selected as crew on a racing yacht is fierce. It's extremely uncomfortable and extremely competitive. Although Terry has used his powers of persuasion to get me onto the boats whenever possible, I am always conscious of being ballast and beholden to the benevolence of the owners, and I don't really enjoy it anyway.

It isn't a spectator sport either. Once offshore, the yachts are out of sight until they return, at the whim of the winds, so they could be gone a day, or three days. There is no way of knowing.

7. The Dog Flew Too

Terry has become our new dad and announces one day that he has decided to give up sailing. Both of us working all week and then spending every summer weekend apart isn't ideal for family life. I do admit I am glad and at the same time guilty. I know how much he loves it.

Soon I don't feel guilty any more, because he finds a new passion.

Flying.

He buys an aeroplane.

Stop right there if you are imagining a 6-seater, twin-engined 200 mph machine upholstered in powder blue leather and containing a cocktail cabinet.

The new family member is a vintage Beagle Pup, a British-built plane that costs less than your average secondhand car. Even I, knowing nothing about aeroplanes, can appreciate the lovely lines of this little aircraft. It is very pretty indeed, in profile like a child's drawing of a whale, seating two in the front and two small ones in the back. On the nose is a life-sized painting of a scantily-dressed woman, with *Susie II* emblazoned beside it.

I'm looking forward to us all being able to go flying around the country once Terry has his licence. He spends every available moment taking lessons from an instructor who needs to earn a living, and only does so when he's instructing, so he can't afford to be deterred by bad weather. When all other aircraft at the airfield are on the ground, in fog, snow, sleet or hail, he and Terry are up in the air. In time, that is going to come in useful because more often than not we'll be flying in terrifying conditions.

Flying is very much more exciting, interesting and warmer than sailing, and it's something the whole family can enjoy, including our dog

Natalya Nightwitch, a Hungarian Vizsla I bought as a puppy for Terry's Christmas present. He has named her after a Russian lady named Natalya Meklin, one of the intrepid Russian female bomber pilots who were known as the night witches. They flew by night, in flimsy wooden aircraft, cutting their engines to glide silently, undetected, to drop their bombs over Germany.

Our Natalya loves the plane, leaping up onto the wing and curling up on the front seat. When it lands she sits up imperiously with her nose in the air as the plane taxies to a halt. She has become quite a celebrity, being introduced to royalty and greeted by people who don't know Terry's name nor mine, but they all know Natalya.

She comes with us to race weekends and has her own racing licence, No. 007½ issued by the Royal Aero Club. At one function when I asked the catering staff if they would open the tin for her lunch, they take it away and return it decorated with a tomato rose, on a silver tray.

Natalya is the object of affection of the air show commentator and aviation artist John Blake, a giant personality with a magnificent handlebar moustache and mutton chop sideburns. He adores her, always welcoming her with a booming 'My DARLING girl!'

John is missing a hand due to an accident with a grenade, and enjoys shocking people by offering his arm to Natalya so it looks as if she has swallowed his hand right up to the elbow.

After John has shared a pint with her, she is slightly tipsy. She is racing with Terry in the afternoon, and as he takes off, she scrambles from the back into the front, breathing beery fumes, and tries to sit on his lap.

Terry says: 'Natalya, get in the back and lie down,' forgetting that he is transmitting over the radio. The incident becomes one of John's favourite tales.

When she is three years old, Natalya produces a litter of eight exquisite baby Vizslas. We keep three. When they are introduced to flying, they all have different reactions. The Grand Wizard aka Wizzie is indifferent; he's very calm by nature and takes everything in his stride. Vulcan, a.k.a. Piggywinkle, doesn't enjoy it at all and tucks himself away in the small luggage compartment behind the rear seats, but their sister Hecate is fascinated. She watches the instruments intently, following every movement of Terry's hands on the joystick and throttle. In a moment of excitement, she claws at the throttle, pulling it back while they are taking off in formation with two other aircraft, and almost causing the plane to stall. Vulcan comforts himself by chewing through the headset cables, leaving Terry without any means of communicating with ground control or other aircraft.

With the English summer weather being what it is, there are weekends when we are grounded and sit in fuggy club houses drinking coffee, getting excited whenever the clouds momentarily part to reveal a chink of blue. Pilots stand outside and glare at the sky as if by the power of their will they can force it into clearing, and convince themselves that it will be OK in half an hour.

Soon Terry isn't satisfied with simply flying circuits or visiting other airfields. He's aerobatting, looping the loop, barrel rolling, doing stall turns and all kinds of horrible manoeuvres with the plane upside down, back to front and inside out. He's competing in streamer cutting competitions which involve throwing toilet rolls out of the window and chopping them up with the propeller blades, flour bombing targets and popping balloons. He's also flying in close formation with other aircraft. I won't be doing any of that that. Ever. I'm a straight-and-level, keep-your-distance flier.

When the Falklands War breaks out, he comes home one day in a state of great excitement, to say he's signed up to go there as a fighter pilot. I never know when he's serious or just pulling my leg, but I say: 'Well, you just go and resign straight away.'

Those days when he is playing daredevil, I stay closer to earth with my beautiful mare Leila, and my daughter Julie on her little grey pony. I have so many memories of peaceful rides through country lanes and exhilarating gallops, with Julie's little voice yelling behind me: 'Mum, are we having roast potatoes for lunch?'

I also have a wonky ring finger, a souvenir of the frosty morning when we are riding near the local golf course. A rabbit leaps out from the bracken, spooking the pony. It shies in fright, depositing Julie on the ground. She is unhurt, and I follow the pony to try to catch it. It has spotted and made a beeline for the nice green grass on the golf course, where it stops to graze. When I am within a couple of yards of it, an infuriated woman runs at it, screaming and waving a golf club. The pony takes off, kicking up divots as it zigzags from one side of the green to the other, attracting more angry golfers. The angrier they get and the more they shout and threaten the pony, the more the pony gallops backwards and forwards in panic, kicking up the turf. I shout at them to let me catch the pony while they shout and curse me to get off the course. Eventually, the pony returns to the path, sweating and steaming, and I can catch its reins. As I do so, it swings behind Leila, twisting my arm. With Julie back on board, we ride home. It isn't until we have untacked and stabled the horses that I notice the top knuckle of my ring finger is bent at right angles to its neighbour, broken and dislocated. It's the only bone I've ever broken, which is remarkable given the number of times I have fallen off horses.

Terry has had the plane for a year when he mentions casually that he has decided to take up air racing, and I will be his navigator. That sounds rather fun. I have assumed that air racing will be in a straight line, from A to B, but learn that is not usually the case. With a few exceptions, the races are run around a circuit of rough squares or rectangles, demarcated on the ground by bright red inflatable cones around which the racing planes turn. We go for a practice flight and do my first and last racing turn.

The plane flicks onto its side, pulling a 90-degree turn so that one wing is pointing up at the sky and the other down at the ground. I am simultaneously paralysed with fear and trying not to vomit. It feels as if we are going to fall out of the sky; my neck is breaking and my stomach has fallen into my throat. I know instantly and with immutable certainty that this is something I am never going to do again. As you already know, I am not in the least intrepid. My sporting activities have been limited to playing netball at school, horse riding ever since and a game of ping pong when the opportunity arises.

Luckily, there is an abundant supply of volunteers eager to take my place, so I step aside graciously and relegate myself to 'supporter'.

Air racing is usually a two-day event held over the weekends at various airfields around the country, throughout the summer. Saturdays are for practice, then the race takes place on Sunday.

We leave on a damp, drizzly Saturday morning for our first air race which is taking place at a small airport in Kent (since closed).

By the time we arrive it's raining hard, but forecast to clear later in the afternoon.

Despite the weather, the pilots are still practising. With their planes grounded, they have improvised and are sitting in luggage trolleys, being pushed by their navigators, whooping and yelling, elbowing, tally-hoing and smashing into each other, with trolleys crashing and turning over. Terry is pushed around by one of the sport's most luminous personalities, and also one of the nicest, Spencer Flack, a motor racing enthusiast as well as an air racer.

Far from being the staid and serious sport I had expected, I realise there and then that everybody involved is completely bonkers. Not only the pilots – the committee members who organise these events are equally crackers.

When somebody puts their head around the door to announce that visibility has cleared and practice is on, the mad race comes to an abrupt end. Abandoning the scattered trolleys, the crews run out and start their engines.

The engines splutter, growl and screech as the planes take off. There's a tiny single-seater that looks like a child's bathtub held up by an umbrella, which sounds like a sewing machine and appears to be barely moving (reminds me of sailing!) alongside vintage aircraft and fast twin-engines with their angry roars. The handicapper's task is to assess the power and speed of each aircraft and start them in such a way that by the end of the race they will all be approaching the finishing line at the same time. The flimsy little things will be first away and will have more than likely almost finished the race before the most powerful planes have taken off.

There are mysterious tweaks that pilots secretly carry out to their engines in the hope of beating the handicapper. The regulations state that if they exceed their declared speed by more than 1% during the race they will be disqualified, so it's quite a balancing act.

I'm impressed by how much alcohol is imbibed over dinner on Saturday evenings. I've had a fair share myself but I am at least able to walk without clinging to someone else, something that not everybody is able to do. I'm even more impressed by how they are all perfectly sober next day.

Watching an air race is both exciting and frightening.

The planes take off one behind the other, spaced apart. The little bathtub/umbrella is first away. It will be starting the final of five laps before the big twins have taken off.

As they tick off the laps, the aircraft begin to close up and bunch together, tipped steeply on their sides as they rack around the turning points, above, below, behind, in front and beside each other like bees in a swarm. They approach the finishing line in a noisy cluster, diving for the last drop of speed they can squeeze from their engines. If the handicapper has done a good job, they will all cross the line within a few seconds of each other.

Air racing is a glamorous and expensive game, so we are lucky that the UK's premier aviation magazine *Fly Past* is sponsoring us, and Ken Ellis, the magazine's editor is Terry's navigator.

It's also a dangerous game, and while there are scares – running low on fuel, engine problems calling for emergency landings, or pilot error leading to near misses – there are mercifully few fatalities. The only one during the years that we went racing occurred in 1984 in Kent.

One of our friends has come along to watch the race. He and I are sitting chatting on the grass waiting for the planes to appear on the final lap when we notice people clustering around the control tower, looking anxiously at the sky. Somebody has signalled a radio message that two aircraft have collided and crashed. The identity of one plane is known, but the other is not.

Twenty-four planes started the race. We know only twenty-two will finish. As they begin to arrive, we watch and wait.

One by one they cross the line. Twenty planes are home; there is no sign of Terry. Everybody is staring silently into the skies. A small smudge comes into sight in the distance. As it nears, we can see it is not Terry. People begin closing around me. I feel sick. Somebody puts a hand around my shoulders.

Nothing happens for what seems like hours. We stand and stare at the sky until at last another smudge appears, seemingly flying in slow motion. It's Terry bringing the plane home with engine problems.

Two popular pilots have lost their lives. If there is any comfort to be taken, it is that both were flying solo and not with passengers. There is no celebration for the race winners.

I remember the years we went air racing as certainly the most fun we ever had. There was a tremendous bond of friendship among all those involved, and there was never a dull moment. It's a sport for swashbucklers and extroverts.

One venue is notorious for wild behaviour. Saturday night is the 'let your hair down' event of the year. Dinner rapidly becomes a riot, with food flying through the air, clothing removed, cutlery orchestras, furniture rearranged and serving staff swept up into the mêlée. I get caught up in the madness and am horrified when the robot takes control again, forcing me to involuntarily push somebody's face into a trifle. It's like the end of term at St Trinian's.

The hotel refuses to accept any future bookings from the club.

However, we are back there the following year, booked in as The Women's Institute by the club secretary, with a plea that we behave ourselves. We do, until dessert arrives with squirty cream. Squirty cream may not be a temptation to the Women's Institute members, but it's a battle cry to air racers. The dining room begins to look like a snow scene.

Suddenly, one of the waitresses screams: 'Oh no! It's THEM!'

Despite their horror, the staff know they will be generously compensated from the proceeds of a collection passed around in a dish, or, as on one occasion, in the hollow prosthetic leg of one of the navigators. The same leg has also been used as an alternative to the starting flag.

Although the humour is generally wild, wacky and noisy, it can also be subtle.

One of the older single pilots has invited a young lady for the weekend to one of the better-behaved venues. He has made a special effort, and is wearing a smart pair of trousers, polished shoes and an expensive jacket. He's freshly shaven and has had his hair cut.

Before dinner we all meet in the bar, and word is passed around telling us to keep an eye on him.

He is chatting to his guest. His hand goes into his jacket pocket to take out a cigarette. He strikes his lighter and takes a drag, before returning the packet of cigarettes and lighter to his pocket. He sniffs his fingers and heads for the bathroom.

He returns, and goes through the same sequence again. He seems to be fascinated by the smell on his fingers, unaware that everybody in the room is covertly watching him and stifling laughter.

After dinner he is still having the same problem, and is now asking other people to sniff his fingers. Those who oblige reel back and wave their hands in front of their face.

Maybe one day he'll find the small blob of Epoisses, probably the world's smelliest cheese, which one of his friends dropped in his pocket. It was the funniest evening we had ever had without breaking anything. And not a fleck of squirty cream to be seen.

(It reminds me of the Tube Theatre in London where we once spent a very amusing evening. Did you ever see it? You booked by phone, and were told to be on the platform of a particular tube station at a specific time and to look out for a man wearing a pinstriped suit, carrying a newspaper and a rolled umbrella. Without appearing to be with him, you followed him on and off trains as he did silly things. He peeled an orange and dropped the peel in the pocket of a lady standing in front of him, and sneakily cut out the crossword puzzle from the newspaper of an unsuspecting man sitting reading opposite. His umbrella hooked into another passenger's pocket causing them to miss their stop. Of course all his 'victims' were stooges and the fun was in watching the reactions of the passengers who didn't realise it was an act. He tried to wrench open the doors on the wrong side of the carriage when it pulled into a station, and struggled to do up his too-long tie, resorting to cutting half of it off with a pair of scissors borrowed from a passenger. He was so clever and ever so funny.)

Back to air racing, the most glamorous event on the air racing calendar is the Schneider Trophy race at Bembridge on the Isle of Wight. There's a gala dinner held on the airfield under a marquee exquisitely decorated with silk and ribbons, hanging plants and dangling chandeliers.

The year after Natalya produced her litter of gorgeous pups, of which we have kept three, the race organisers ask us to bring them all to Bembridge to be included in a documentary film.

We have all been booked into a holiday camp on the island for the Friday and Saturday nights. The camp is very *Hi-de-Hi!* and rather tired, but the only place with sufficient capacity to accommodate us all in the same place. It's one of those establishments where you have to order your breakfast at 6.00 pm the previous evening, and where the earnest youth at the reception greets an Admiral of the Fleet Air Arm, who races the Royal Navy Chipmunk, as 'mate'.

Our room is minuscule, with less than two feet between the door and the end of the bed, one foot each side of the bed, and the kettle and tea tray are perched on top of the wardrobe, so you will have to stand on the bed to reach it. With the four dogs, it's quite a squeeze.

We are woken late at night by management insisting that we leave because they do not allow dogs. Somebody has complained and will not be satisfied until we are removed. This turns out very well, as the club secretary organises alternative accommodation for us at a small hotel in the town where we are given a magnificent room with a four-poster bed.

With racing, aerobatting and social visits to other airfields, *Susie II* works hard during the summer. There's also our annual trip to Europe with other members of the aircraft club, exploring new airfields where we usually camp.

The prettiest airfield we find is at Gruyères, nestled in a flowery Swiss meadow surrounded by mountains. We set up camp among the buttercups, and then take a taxi into the exquisite little medieval town to enjoy a cup of coffee and a blueberry tart. The coffee is well worth its astronomical price. Served in a large cup, it comes accompanied by a little jug of rich yellow cream. The little jug is made of chocolate and when lowered into the cup it melts languorously, releasing a lazy swirl of cream.

You can't go on holiday to Switzerland without having a fondue, and in Gruyères the melted cheese is accompanied by a wooden bucket filled with small boiled potatoes. I feel I could eat it for every meal, every day for the rest of my life. Heaven.

However, even camping in Switzerland is prohibitively expensive, so next day we fly back into France, landing at a small airfield just as everybody is going home for lunch. The club members leave the clubhouse and bar unlocked and ask us to help ourselves. If we leave before they return, just make a note of what we have drunk and leave a payment on the bar.

We find this at every small airfield we visit, hospitality and trust.

One year as a change from camping we decide to rent a holiday home near Libourne airfield in the Gironde. It's very basic, as *gîtes* used to be in those days. A notice on the door warns guests not to touch any of the electric switches with our hands as the wiring is dangerous. Long pieces of wood are at our disposal to push the switches up and down. There are chalk marks upstairs outlining places where the floorboards are rotten, and treading on them will risk plummeting through to the floor below.

The bedrooms are extremely primitive, as is the kitchen, and another pinned notice says it is our obligation to mow the grass with the ancient mower.

Even with its little idiosyncrasies, it's a more comfortable option and makes a change from camping on an airfield. The weather is superb, there's a bakery two minutes away and a number of good restaurants close by.

Rather unfortunately, we soon find that sharing a house with a mix of people is not the same as having a meal with them every so often. Whereas we have all agreed to share the costs of shopping and meals out equally, one couple will only pay for precisely what they eat and drink, using a pocket calculator to refine it down to the last centime. The men expect the women to do all the cooking and clearing up while they relax, and one of the men refuses to take his turn driving the hired car because he is on holiday. There are squabbles over who is eating and drinking more than their share.

By the end of the week, the atmosphere is strained and we are all looking forward to leaving. Most people go their separate ways – we will meet up again soon and have put it all behind us, our friendships undamaged – while we and a couple of friends head back north on our way home.

We are within an hour of the French coast when the weather falls down upon us. Rolling black clouds reduce visibility to almost nil, so we find the nearest airfield and land there. We ask at the club house if we may pitch the tents which we carry in the plane. They agree, so we unpack them and begin putting them up. The wind picks up, and the rain comes down in a sudden surge, almost blowing the tents out of our hands and into the rapidly developing mud. As we battle to secure them, somebody runs out from the club house, telling us to bring our things inside and stay there overnight. The weather, he says, will be clear tomorrow, but for tonight we are welcome to shelter inside.

We haul our bags and mattresses through the rain into the club house as the members go home, leaving the bar unlocked and the coffee machine switched on.

We are warm and dry, but we don't have any food, not a crumb, so we consult the telephone directory and search in vain for a local taxi. As far as we can see, there isn't one.

The rain dwindles from torrential to just unpleasant and we start walking towards the town. It probably isn't much more than a mile, but against a strong wind and driving drizzle it seems to take forever. None of us has any rain gear. It's almost 7.00 pm, and we last ate at breakfast. We are very hungry and rather irritable as we plod along the road, becoming progressively wetter and hungrier.

When we reach the town, we wander the dismal streets in search of somewhere we can buy food. Signs point to a hotel, which is closed. The kebab shop is closed. The bakery is closed. There are no people to be seen. It is like a ghost town. Increasingly despondent, we trudge around peering down dark alleys. I am on the verge of tears, I am so hungry.

We decide to head back to the airfield and see if we can find any chocolate or packets of peanuts in the bar to keep us going until next morning. Turning a corner, suddenly we spot a light in the window of a dingy building at the end of the street, with a sign above the door saying it is a restaurant. We run towards it in case it closes before we can get there, shouting to each other that whoever reaches it first must burst in and refuse to leave until we are fed.

The floor and walls of the reception area are covered in a grey-green, moss-like carpet; on the counter an enormous decorative cabbage perches precariously on an alabaster vase. There are two people there: a woman with ticker-tape stuck all over her face and a portly man with a big smile, wearing a black T-shirt bearing a luminous image of a skyline and the words 'I Love Manhattan'.

Were we not cold, wet, footsore and crazed with hunger we would turn around and walk out, but as we are, we ask: 'Are you serving dinner?'

They were, and the ticker-tape-faced lady beckons us to a table in a small dining area. The man who loves Manhattan hops and skips to the table, flourishing a menu which offers a surprising variety of dishes. Our companions both order the roast lamb, while we choose the trout. Mr

Manhattan plonks a large carafe of red wine and a basket of bread on the table, then bounces off towards the kitchen.

A group of four noisy people are the only other guests. They appear to be well into their cups and extremely friendly, waving and shouting out to '*les rosbifs*'.

We have worked our way through the carafe of wine and basket of bread when the food arrives in brown paper bags, much to our surprise, none of us having ever seen lamb or trout cooked in this fashion. Still, by now we are prepared to eat anything, even brown paper bags.

Opening them reveals red mullet *en papillote*, which Manhattan man explains is the only dish they are serving this evening. We do wonder why he has given us a menu and waited for us to choose dishes that are not available, but the fish is delicious, we mop the juice up with the bread, and a second carafe of red wine arrives with a *baguette* and some cheese.

The ticker-tape lady pulls up a chair and joins us, explaining in near-perfect English the reason she is wearing ticker-tape. She fell down an escalator in Paris a few days ago and broke her nose. The ticker-tape is some kind of medical bandage holding her nose in shape. Helping herself to *baguette* and cheese, she asks how we came to be in this, as she herself says, gloomy part of the country. Once the town was a busy textile industry, but since it closed down there is nothing left. Most shops and restaurants have gone. She says that although this is the best restaurant in the town, and the food is excellent, local people won't come because the owner is gay. They don't like gay people and believe they will contract AIDS if they eat here.

While she is talking, one of the noisy people from the other table comes and puts a bottle of champagne on the table, ignoring our protests and insisting it is a pleasure to welcome *les rosbifs*.

A little later the Manhattan-loving owner/chef joins us. Flamboyant is an understatement. He walks with an exaggerated swing of the hips, his hands fluttering at shoulder height like wings, and sinks down onto a chair wiping his brow theatrically.

'It's over. That's enough. I can't go on any longer,' he laments.

A ghostly white man with ghostly white hair appears from the kitchen and shuffles over to him in shapeless bedroom slippers and bends to whisper in his ear. Manhattan man waves him away with a flick of his hand, and the ghostly white man disappears slowly back through the kitchen door.

We sit in silence for a few minutes, before Manhattan gives a great sigh and says: 'He's too old and boring. All he wants to do is sit and watch television. I want to go dancing and enjoy life. I need to find a new man.'

We murmur sympathetically.

The noisy people from the other table come and sit with us, and produce two more bottles of champagne which they insist on sharing. Manhattan man asks if we want a *digestif*, and we ask if there is any Cointreau. No, but they do have Grand Marnier somewhere. Ticker-tape goes behind the bar and finds a full bottle – a large bottle – and fills our wineglasses to the brim. By now, we have drunk so much that common sense and inhibitions have evaporated. We try to converse with our new friends, only one of whom – Ticker-tape – speaks English, and amongst us I'm the only one who can speak more than half a dozen words of French. It doesn't seem to matter because we all just keep laughing and drinking Grand Marnier, and I think there was another bottle of champagne too.

Time ticks away, as it does, and even in our state we remember we are quite far from the airfield, having no idea which direction it is in. We ask if one of our new friends can help us find a taxi. They confirm, as we have already discovered, that there are no taxis in the town.

We explain that we have walked from the airfield and don't know how to get back. A very pretty, tiny girl who tells us she is a dentist says she will take us in her car. She will give her three companions a lift, as it is once again pouring with rain.

The bill, when it comes, is only for the fish. Everything else is either on the house, or paid for by our noisy new friends.

When our lift arrives, it's a Citroën 2CV, the tiny iconic little French car designed to carry four people. As there are eight of us, we have a brief discussion as to whether the dentist will ferry us in two shifts, but she insists we can all fit in. Three squash into the front next to her, and four of us into the back, moulded to each other like pieces of a jigsaw puzzle. Despite being drunk, she manages to steer through the unlit streets without hitting anything, and delivers us in one piece back to the airfield, refusing to accept any payment.

The club house has been left unlocked for us so we are able to bed down on the floor in our sleeping bags for what is left of the night.

Next morning, the weather has cleared but our tents are still saturated so it takes several hours for them to be dry enough to pack into the aircraft. A member of the club drives to town and buys a bag of croissants for our breakfast. Anybody who thinks the French are inhospitable and xenophobic should visit that little town.

There's a strong wind when we take off, and the plane bounces around. Suffering from a hangover and feeling very unwell, all I can think of is a plate of chips with salt and vinegar. At Cherbourg, we land sideways on the runway, buffeted by the wind. There are no chips there so I make do with a dry bread roll.

After we have taken off again to cross the channel, the aircraft radio has stopped working. Drawing alongside the other plane, Terry makes a 'cutting the throat' signal to tell them we are without radio contact and will follow them. That is all well and good until we approach the British coast, when we are suddenly surrounded by thick cloud and almost no visibility. Consequently, we are dependent upon the other aircraft and have to fly alongside them, almost touching their wing tips. Any lasting effect of the alcohol is replaced with gut-clenching fear on my part. I hate being so close to another aircraft, I hate not being able to see the ground, I hate having no means of contact with air traffic control, I hate being so frightened and I am aware that if we lose sight of the other plane, we are in very serious trouble because we can neither see where we are nor hear any instructions from the ground.

We are expecting the leading plane to begin an approach to land, but instead it begins circling, round and round, so close to us, round and round and round in circles. As close as we are, it is still almost invisible among the thick grey cloud. For some reason, we have been put on hold by air traffic control. It is very quiet in the cockpit, Terry concentrating fiercely on maintaining contact with the vague shadow of the other plane, and me beginning to wonder if it is too late to adopt a religion.

Obviously, we do eventually land safely, otherwise I wouldn't be writing this. It was one of many very hairy moments spent in horrible weather conditions, and for which we remain eternally grateful to Terry's intrepid instructor for all those lessons in perilous weather.

8. Lost in France

We are due to leave on our annual club outing to France, but *Susie II* has been resprayed and her paint is not quite dry at our appointed mid-morning departure time. We will follow on later in the day, and catch up with our fellow flyers at the first destination, Bordeaux.

It is after 4.00 pm by the time the paint is dry, and off we set into a cloudless blue sky. Loosely speaking, I am the navigator, sitting holding a very large, crackly, plasticised map covered with china-graph pencil marks. Once we've crossed the Channel – always a slightly unnerving episode when the engine invariably sounds rough and you wonder how long it would take to clamber out when the plane falls into the water – we are pleasantly relaxed, cruising along and looking forward to a good meal when we reach Bordeaux in three hours time.

The cumbersome map is redundant as we are following a navigational beacon, so I tuck it out of the way and drowse in the pleasant warmth of the cockpit with the sun on my face.

I suddenly become aware that the sun has disappeared and the sky has clouded over. On the horizon, there is a wall of black cloud. We are heading into a storm.

'I'm not flying into that!' I say. Flying through thunder and lightning is strictly for adrenaline junkies, one of which I am not. We have already done it out of necessity enough times for me to know that it is a horrible, frightening experience.

'OK,' says Terry, 'we'll land at the next airfield. Where are we?'

'I thought you knew.'

'No, I'm following a beacon. You're meant to be watching the map. Tell me where we are and find the nearest airfield.'

I unfold the crinkly, crackly map and stare at it, trying to find landmarks on the ground to relate to those on the map. I see a railway line, a river, a town, a motorway and a runway. Calculating the distance we would have covered in the time we've been flying, it all makes sense, even if the terrain doesn't precisely correspond to the map. I name the town where I think we are.

As the black band of weather surges closer, we circle until Terry spots the airfield, which is not quite where the map puts it, but who cares at this moment? It's a runway.

He lines up for the approach, and we touch down on a particularly wide and long runway marked with a great deal of white paint. The wheels bump gently onto the tarmac, making a funny noise and giving a little shudder. We roll to a halt. Terry switches off the engine then climbs out and crouches down to look under the plane. He walks around to my side, and says:

'We have a problem. We've landed on a military airfield.'

'Is that bad?'

'Yes.'

'Let's just fly quickly away,' I suggest, as a *gendarme* cycles towards us and climbs off his bike.

'Hello,' he says, in perfect English. 'Why are you here?'

'We made a precautionary landing due to approaching bad weather,' Terry says.

We all gaze up the sky, which is now crystal clear without a wisp of a cloud.

'You should fly quickly away,' advises the *gendarme*, confirming my suggestion, 'because otherwise you will be in a lot of trouble. You must go now.'

'We have a damaged wheel.' indicates Terry. 'We can't take off.'

'Oh, *la vache!*' exclaims the *gendarme*. 'If you can get your plane the other side of this fence, it is the aero club, but the entrance is locked. It will be very bad if the military find you here.'

A large camouflaged truck comes speeding towards us and parks itself on the nose of the plane. Out spring half a dozen camouflage-clad soldiers with guns, and a German shepherd dog wearing a camouflaged muzzle. The soldiers surround the plane, pointing their guns at it and us. The dog stands and stares.

The *gendarme* explains to them what we have said, and then he turns to us. 'I am sorry for your problem. It is a military matter now. Good luck.' He climbs onto his bike and cycles away.

My French is fairly limited, while Terry knows '*bonjour*', '*s'il vous plaît*', '*merci*' '*vin*' and '*fromage*'.

One of the soldiers speaks a little English. He enquires what we are doing on a military airfield. With vague gestures and a few words of Franglais we explain about the approaching storm. All eyes turn up to a sky devoid of any hint of cloud.

A large car sweeps along the tarmac and comes to a halt beside us. Out from the back steps a man in mess uniform, looking as irritable and arrogant as only a French Air Force officer can when his dinner has been interrupted. There is a universal code of camaraderie among pilots, but the officer seems unaware of it. He ignores us completely and snaps at one of the soldiers.

'This officer is going to taxi your aircraft into a hangar.' explains the English-speaking soldier.

'He is not!' replies Terry. 'He is not to touch my plane.'

'But he is an officer of the French Air Force,' stutters the English-speaker.

'I don't care who or what he is. This is a British aircraft, and he is not to touch it.'

The English-speaker translates to the officer who stalks back to his car, slams the door, and is driven away.

A van arrives with two *gendarmes*, who invite us into it. One of them has a very oddly shaped head, like a clothes peg. It is flat on top and at the back, and runs seamlessly into his neck and shoulders. They drive us to a large, sinister building with lots of doors and gates, telephones, red lights and machines making pinging noises.

An officer questions us in halting English. We give our explanation in halting French. He shakes his head and picks up a telephone. After a brief conversation, he tells us that we are being handed over to the police.

Back we climb into the *gendarmes'* van, and are driven at terrifying speed through a small town to a police station. There we are taken into an office and introduced to an exasperated policeman who speaks not a single word of English. He puts his head in his hands, takes a deep breath and summons another policeman, speaking rapidly while jerking a finger at us. The only word I can recognise is '*Anglais*'.

The second policeman disappears and returns five minutes later with an interpreter – one of the prisoners, a smiling gentleman from Senegal wearing a fetching pale lavender and white shell suit.

With a line of communication established, the policeman asks yet again why we have chosen to land on a French military airfield. Once again, we explain that we had seen a storm approaching.

The policeman takes out from his drawer a large book with cartoon-like drawings in it. It appears to be a policeman's manual of how to deal with any eventuality.

An old lady falling under a bus.

A bicycle in a ditch.

A car on its back.

A burglar climbing out of a window.

He flicks through the pages searching in vain for a drawing of a British aircraft landing on a French military airfield.

He takes a notebook and a pencil, then with the help of the prisoner/interpreter, begins writing.

He notes our passport numbers, our address in England, and the registration letters of the aircraft.

'What is your aero club?' he asks.

Terry is just about to give the name and telephone number of our local flying club, when he recalls that it is Saturday evening. On Saturday evenings, the club members who, even on quiet weekdays are as mad as a box of frogs, will be smashed out of their heads. We can visualise the scene in the clubhouse, people smacking each other around the head with barstools, and knickers hanging from the propeller above the bar. The telephone will ring. A heavily-accented French voice will ask whether we are club members. Entering into the spirit of the thing, whoever answers the phone will adopt a Peter Sellers accent and say that *oui, oui,* we are well-known drug smugglers, dangerous and likely to be carrying concealed firearms.

He has a quick rethink.

'The Royal Aero Club,' he replies.

'Who is the President of your club?'

'Prince Andrew.'

'Who is he?'

'He is the son of Her Majesty Queen Elizabeth, who is the patron of the club.'

He puts down his pencil with a sigh.

'We will take you to a hotel for tonight.' he says. 'How much money do you have?'

Enough to sustain us modestly for a week. Not enough to stay in the George V.

'Very little,' I reply.

Thanking the prisoner/translator for his services, we are put back into the police van and taken to a strange building, a kind of rickety corrugated iron and wooden shed at the back of a railway siding. Inside. about two dozen drunken French people sit at trestle tables, arms linked, swaying and singing merrily. They give us a friendly wave and invite us to join them. We sit at the table smiling foolishly.

The beaming *patronne* plants two gigantic plates of *charcuterie* in front of us. We shake our heads. Back she comes ten minutes later with some chicken and rice. '*Volaille,*' she smiles. We point at the chicken and shake our heads. The singers have stopped and are watching us curiously, murmuring amongst themselves.

'Omelette?' asks the *patronne*. When we nod, there is a collective and audible sigh of relief. She comes back in a few minutes with the biggest – I estimate a dozen eggs in each – and very best omelettes we have ever tasted.

The singers seem to be performing an Edith Piaf tribute, and although they are all patently drunk as skunks, they sing beautifully. It is one of the strangest places we have eaten, but also one of the most charming.

Because of our abrupt transfer from the plane to the interrogation unit at the airfield, we have nothing with us apart from Terry's wallet. No change of clothes, no toothpaste, nothing.

Our hostess leads us to a bedroom which resides behind the urinals and seems to be constructed out of compacted cardboard. There are three double beds, all made up with brushed cotton sheets that have obviously been slept in many times. One has a large coffee stain all over it. The sheets have gone bobbly, and each bobble had a small black dot in it, like an embryonic tadpole in frogspawn. The aroma from the urinals is overpowering. We select the least dirty bed, use our arms as pillows and fall asleep fully dressed to the stirring sounds of '*La Foulè*'.

Next morning, we are up at daybreak, keen to breathe clean air. We stroll into the town and find a lively market where we wander around enjoying the sights, sounds and smells of our first full day in France. We buy a kilo of cherries and a large punnet of strawberries, then find a café where we sit munching croissants, sipping *grandes crèmes* and wondering what is going to happen next. In the distance, we notice two *gendarmes* frantically trotting around, peering into shops, obviously searching for us. We wave to them and they gallop over, panting and relieved that we have not escaped.

After we have settled the tiny bill for our excellent omelettes and unspeakable bed, the *gendarmes* hurtle us back to the airfield, where a friendly French Air Force officer shakes hands. He is also a private pilot, and speaks perfect English. He has been summonsed from Beauvais airport to get to the bottom of why we have chosen to land uninvited at a French military airfield. Once again, we mention the ominous weather that had appeared suddenly and disappeared equally suddenly, and the officer says that he did recall that a band of bad weather had swept quickly through the area the previous evening. We are vindicated and free to leave.

But of course we cannot. As I mentioned earlier, the aircraft has a broken wheel.

That is no problem. With a metaphorical click of his fingers, our new friend summons a fleet of French Air Force engineers, who remove the wheel, take it away and return it repaired a couple of hours later. There is no charge. Having being suspected enemies of the State the previous day, we are now cherished friends. As we prepare to fly away, a crowd gathers. The two policeman from the van; the *gendarme* and his bicycle from the previous day; the officer from Beauvais and the team of engineers. After they have all shaken hands with Terry and kissed me, we take off and circle their military airfield overhead, whereupon Terry points the nose down and we swoop over them. From the ground, our French friends wave and cheer. They seem to be pointing at something. Glancing through the side window, I see the plastic bags of cherries and strawberries dangling from the exterior step into the plane, just before they slide off and away into space.

Once back in England, we recount our adventure to some friends, and remark that the arrival of one small British plane seemed to have caused a disproportionate reaction by the French military.

'You were lucky,' remarks one of them. 'You could have been shot down.'

We laugh. The likelihood that the French Air Force would blow a tiny private aircraft out of the air is remote. We could hardly have been seen as a threat to their national security.

Subsequently, we hear that shortly before our adventure, an English civil servant had fooled the owner of an aircraft for sale, handing him a briefcase full of bank notes in a cash payment for the plane. By the time the owner realised the briefcase was actually filled with Monopoly money, the plane had flown away. It flew across the Channel and into France where it was picked up on French radar, heading for Paris. The pilot was not responding to radio messages warning him that if he penetrated Paris air-space he would be shot down. Two fighter planes were launched to guide him out of the area and force him to land. The airfield where his adventure came to a forced ending was Creil, which by pure coincidence is exactly the same airfield at which we landed.

9. Once is Too Much

Terry has a call from a friend living a hundred miles away, asking him to deliver a painting they have bought. The weather is fine and it's a welcome opportunity for him to use the plane, so he arranges to meet his friend at their nearest airfield.

When flying from one place to another, the pilot has to file a flight plan stating where they are going. Terry files the plan stating his destination.

Part way on his journey the weather clamps down just before a range of hills, so as a precaution he lands at the nearest available airfield and waits for the weather to clear.

While he's at the deserted airstrip, he decides to change the plane's paper oil filter, and having done so needs to dispose of it, which he does by tucking it discreetly into a hedge where it will decompose.

Once the weather has lifted, he takes off and heads towards his destination, where he lands, meets his friend and goes to have a coffee in the clubhouse.

Ten minutes later, a vehicle arrives with Customs officers and a sniffer dog. They approach Terry and say that they have reason to believe he is smuggling drugs. He has landed at an airfield that was not mentioned on his flight plan and was seen hiding something in the hedge. Disregarding his explanation that he made a precautionary landing due to poor visibility, they proceed to thoroughly search the plane. Despite the best efforts of the dog, they find no trace of drugs.

Somewhat peevishly they leave with a warning that they'll be keeping an eye on his movements.

He phones me to explain what has happened, and says that it's possible I will have a visit from Customs. They may want to search the house, so I tidy the kitchen and sweep the floors just in case.

Worn out from the stress of having to do housework, I am pouring a cup of coffee when my heart gives a little jump. I spill scalding liquid on my hand when I suddenly remember that we actually have cannabis in the house.

It has been there for six years, since a musician friend gave it to us when he came to dinner.

'This is the best you can get,' he said, handing us a small packet wrapped in silver foil. We were too polite to reply that neither of us do drugs.

I had dropped it in a drawer, intending to throw it away, and given it no more thought until today.

Just in case we are going to experience a drugs bust, I dig out the little packet from where it has lain tucked away with fuses, pieces of string, the little felt pads you stick under the legs of chairs, duct tape and super glue.

I have never taken any kind of drug in my life, not because of any other reason than it has never interested or appealed to me, but looking at it, I wonder idly what it is that people enjoy about the stuff. I've heard that people bake it in cakes and biscuits, so I decide to try that to satisfy my curiosity.

I prepare a batch of almond spoon-handle biscuits. You make a dough, with added almond essence, roll it into balls, flatten them slightly and then stick the handle of a wooden spoon into them to make a depression. It's one of the easiest recipes and a favourite of mine.

I crumble up the cannabis paste and mix it into the dough, then prepare the biscuits and put them in the oven.

When they come out twenty minutes, later they smell delicious. While they are still warm, I eat one, and then another. I put the rest aside until Terry returns home, and after dinner we eat some more.

Between us we finish them all, and then I find myself giggling for no reason. Giggling becomes hysterical laughter, which in turn makes me laugh even more, knowing that I'm laughing for no good reason.

Then the room begins to tilt and swirl. I feel very sick, so I go to bed and spend the night having panic attacks and hallucinations.

By next morning, I am really out of it, unable to focus, having palpitations and feeling terrified, but we are due at an air race, so I get in the plane and spend the flight with my eyes closed. When we arrive at the airfield, one of my friends comes up to greet me, and stops in her tracks.

'Are you OK?' she asks. 'You are a very strange colour.'

I tell her what I've done, and she says I should go and lie down because it will take time for it to pass.

I go to our room and lie on the bed. The wall is tilted inwards, my head is spinning and I'm certain that I am going to die. In fact, I am hoping that I will, because I have never felt so ill and frightened in my life. My mind is a muddled mess.

I stay in bed all night and most of the following day, moaning. Friends come to visit but I don't want to see anybody. I can't put a sentence together.

When I emerge after the race, I look at myself in the mirror and see an ashen face and staring eyes. The whole weekend has passed; I've missed all the fun and all the meals. I've no idea who won the race and I don't care at all. I just want to be at home.

I baked and ate the little cakes on a Thursday. It is the following Wednesday before I feel back to normal. Over that week, I learned everything I would ever want to know about cannabis. And what's more, I've never been able to eat spoon-handle biscuits since then.

10. Help Yourself

On a weekend trip to France, our return home is delayed by atrocious weather. We are marooned in Burgundy in the pretty town of Beaune, with just enough money to pay for fuel for the homeward journey and a cheap hotel for the night, with £20 left for a meal for three of us.

We wander despondently around the streets in the rain and wind looking for somewhere we can afford. The bakeries and shops are all closed and we don't even have a packet of sweets between us. We come upon a small restaurant with a menu in the window that seems ridiculously cheap for a three-course meal. Hesitantly, we walk in and are led down some stone steps into a cosy cellar of exposed stone with a mirrored wall at each end.

We read through the menu. Julie, who is a notoriously fussy eater, declares she doesn't like anything, but once she understands it's this or nothing, she reluctantly chooses a starter and main course and entertains herself preening in the mirrors.

The food is extraordinarily good. If anybody had told me that poached egg in red wine sauce (*œufs en Meurette*) was delicious I would have thought they were pulling my leg, but tonight I'm convinced. The quality of the food seems far beyond the scope our budget. We begin to think we have misunderstood and will spend the early hours of the morning washing up to pay for our meal, but I check with our friendly waiter who confirms that we have correctly understood the price.

We can even afford a small bottle of wine and have sufficient change left from our English £20 to leave a tip for the waiter.

The reason I remember it so well is not only because of the quality and value of the food, nor the attractive setting, but because of one of the waiters.

Terry and I are sitting facing the stairs leading to the kitchen upstairs. There is a particular waiter who looks no older than sixteen. He undertakes his duties with flair and flamboyance, spinning in circles as he makes his way to the tables and serving the dishes with an exaggerated bow. Because he is so amusing, we watch him as he prances down the stairs, skilfully balancing a tray on one hand while the other hand selects choice morsels from the customers' plates and pops them into his mouth.

11. Samos – Learning the Bus

During a particularly bleak English winter, we sit reading the Sunday newspapers on yet another wet day, looking at images of golden beaches, tanned bodies, plates of cheese and olives, and small fishing boats bobbing in blue waters. We decide to take a holiday in Greece.

Knowing nothing about Greece, we book a package tour through a well-known travel company, choosing the island of Samos, which has its own airport so that we will reach our destination with a minimum of travel arrangements.

Six weeks later, we are aboard the coach from the airport to our hotel 'nestling in a grove of pine trees less than a mile from the port, with sea views from the balcony' of our double room – according to the brochure.

The hotel is a modern building which, far from nestling in a grove of pine trees, nestles on the inside of a hairpin bend on a steep hill on the main road leading to the harbour. Non-stop heavy vehicles grind through their gears as they negotiate the tight turn. There is not a tree in sight. Our double room is actually a single room with a double bed crammed into it, forcing us to step onto it in order to get into the room. There is no balcony, and no sea view.

A brief conversation with our holiday hostess, asking for the name of the company's Chief Executive soon puts that right, and we are swiftly transferred into a double room with a double bed and the promised balcony and sea view.

Walking the short distance down to the harbour for our evening meal, surrounded by the noises of the busy port and the warm night air scented with the fragrance of Greek food cooking, we fall in love with Greece. It seems wonderfully foreign and exotic.

Restaurants spill out over the pavements from one side of the road to the other, and waiters skip through the traffic to take and deliver orders. As we are standing deciding where to eat, a waiter bearing a tray with a basket of bread, a little bowl of olives and a carafe of white wine scoops us up with one arm and pirouettes us to a table, laying the contents of the tray in front of us.

He hands us a menu which is all in Greek, illustrated with garish, rather fuzzy photos to give us a rough indication of what we are ordering.

Next to our table is a German family who know Samos well. They recommend an unspoilt beach further along the coast, which we can reach by bus. Take food and something to drink, they say, as there's nothing there. The bus station is behind the church and the bus leaves at about 10.00 am.

When the bill arrives for our meal, there is no mention of the bread, olives or the excellent carafe of local Samos wine. The waiter brushes aside our efforts to pay. It's a gift, he smiles. That ensures our loyalty for the whole of our stay. We eat there every evening.

Next morning, we buy a bottle of wine, a bunch of grapes, some peaches, feta cheese and tender Greek bread sprinkled with onion seeds. We find the bus station in a sweltering square behind the church. The ticket office is in a small dark room. The ticket seller there shakes his head and points to the nearest bus, flapping his hand to indicate that we should just get on it. When we do the driver holds out his hand, takes a few coins we offer him and personally conducts us to our seats.

There does not appear to be a timetable for the bus. It leaves once it's full. Most of our fellow passengers are holidaymakers. This first drive is a magical mystery tour for us. There is no indication anywhere as to the route taken or where the bus stops. It is also a mystery how the driver sees where he is going, as the windscreen is festooned with icons, religious pictures, a couple of notices in Greek and clutches of small, coloured furry bobbles that swing and dance to the movement of the vehicle. There is almost no empty space on the windscreen.

After hauling up the hill out of town, the bus follows the road along the coast. When it stops, I ask a Dutch girl sitting behind us which stop this is.

'Kokkari,' she replies. 'If you're going to the beach, it's the next stop.'

When the bus begins to slow again, people stand up and move to the front. There is no bus stop marked, just a place where the road widens slightly. We follow them over the road and down a steep rocky path through the trees, until we reach the beach of Tsamadou (rhymes with Xanadu where Kubla Khan did his stately pleasure dome build).

In my mind, I had an image of the golden sandy beach like those in the travel brochure, so at first sight this one is a shock. It's carpeted in flat, smooth pebbles so hot you could fry eggs on them if you happened to have eggs to fry. However, once we have got used to them, I prefer them to sand. They don't stick to or intrude into your clothing, or between your toes, and you can shuffle them around to make quite a comfy place to lie down.

The beach occupies a small bay curving around the clearest waters we have ever seen. Small fish flick around in the shallows, nibbling at our feet; a little further out the waters become progressively more blue, from aquamarine to sapphire. There are no more than 20 other people here, and none of them are wearing any clothes.

We spread out our towels, take off our clothes and lay down to bake. The heat is ferocious, and by contrast the waters are icy, so we regularly move back and forth between the two.

A short distance from us are a couple with their pet canary in a fancy cage covered with a small parasol. There is not a square inch of natural shade available, but we manage to poke two corners of one of our towels into the rock face behind us and prop it up with a couple of branches to fashion a crude shelter. We haven't been there long when a naked couple come over and ask if they may join us.

Annie is French, as curvy as a cherub, with dark curly hair. Stamatis is Greek, tall and thin with blond ringlets. They both speak perfect English. Stamatis points at our shopping bag and remarks that in the heat everything will be baked, but he has a solution. In the shallow water, he builds a small circular wall of pebbles and places the bottle in it, then ties the plastic bag handles into a loop that he fixes around the neck of the bottle.

We are sitting chatting when Stamatis says: 'Quickly, cover up!' We wrap our towels around ourselves and notice that all the other people on the beach are doing the same.

A helicopter sweeps around the headland and flies low across the bay.

'Police,' Stamatis says. 'It is forbidden to be naked on the beach, because it could offend people. But everybody on the beach is naked. Maybe they just like to look,' he laughs.

Sometimes, he says, a local policeman comes to the beach to make sure everybody is suitably dressed. But as he has to descend the same steep rocky path as everybody else, slithering down and disturbing small stones that bounce around noisily forewarning everybody of his arrival, there are no naked people when he arrives, so he will stay and share a glass of wine before clambering back up to the road.

Apart from one trip to the capital, Pythagorion, we spend every day at the beach with our new friends. They are easy company, and we can sit for long periods without speaking, simply enjoying the peace and heat, or talk for hours about everything and nothing. They live locally, and are interested to hear what is happening around the world.

When we notice people collecting their things and climbing back up the hill, we follow, and stand in a group waiting for the bus to come. When it does, it hurtles past on the rock-strewn dusty road without stopping. Our fellow travellers explain that some bus drivers do not approve of people going to Tsamadou beach as it is known that people take off their clothes there, so a disapproving driver will not stop. There should be another bus in about an hour, but there is no guarantee that there will be, or that it will stop, so we all walk the mile and a half to Kokkari where there is an official bus stop.

For the same reason, we learn that when we catch the bus from Samos in the morning, we should never mention that we are going to Tsamadou, as some drivers will say that they don't go there.

Armed with that useful tip, next morning we climb onto the same bus we took yesterday, but the driver directs us to the ticket office, the same ticket office which yesterday said we should buy our tickets on the bus. We never do manage to understand the system, if there is one. Each morning, it's trial and error, like the return journey in the evening, where we learn to work out whether or not the bus is going to stop by the amount of dust it's throwing up. Heavy dust clouds mean it's travelling too quickly to pick us up, and so we walk to Kokkari. It is part of the fun and charm of our first Greek holiday.

A very excited Stamatis greets us. 'I have a special gift for you,' he says, producing from behind his back a beautiful golden sponge the size of a newborn baby. My first thought is 'How on earth will we be able to fit it into our suitcase?'

It is a wonderful work of nature, which Stamatis found on the beach earlier this morning. While we are admiring it, there is a shout from nearby as a naked man runs towards us, furiously waving his arms. He tries to snatch the sponge from Stamatis, who clutches it to his chest and clings on with all his strength. The two men shout and wrestle until the other man succeeds in pulling the sponge away and stalks back to the other end of the beach.

Stamatis walks into the sea and sits mournfully on a large rock for the rest of the morning. I ask Annie what it's all about. The other man claims he found the sponge when he was diving and left it on the beach. When Stamatis found it, he thought it had been washed up. The original owner accuses him of stealing, and Stamatis is very upset indeed. I go out to the rock to comfort him, but it seems his masculinity has been severely damaged and he wants to be left alone.

He does cheer up when we have lunch, although he later goes to the sponge owner and has words with him, coming back with a face like thunder.

On the final morning of our holiday, we have arranged to meet up as usual with Annie and Stamatis to share a picnic. We stroll down to the bus station. It's vanished. Where it stood yesterday, and all the days before, is now a car park. The ticket office is closed.

We wander around for a few minutes, asking in my extremely limited Greek where the buses are.

'Behind there,' says everybody I ask, waving a hand towards the church.

'Behind the church,' says the Tourist Office.

'Behind the church,' says the policeman.

We march about in growing frustration. Eventually, we see a bus wending its way up the hill out of Samos from a small alley further up the road, pursued by a crowd of people running behind it, waving their arms and yelling.

Weaving our way through the back streets, guided by an almighty uproar of shouts and bangs and whistles, we find several buses lined up in a narrow lane, blocking all traffic in every direction.

We join a large crowd of extremely angry people, workers, holidaymakers, old ladies all in black, a thin man with two goats on string, somebody with a wicker basket of chickens. They have surrounded a sweating man wearing a vest and a frightened expression. He waggles his arms in the air, trying to make himself heard over the people yelling, banging and kicking the buses parked nose-to-tail in the alley.

The man in the vest spreads out his arms in a futile attempt to form a barrier, but we are not for turning. Everybody scrambles aboard and sits, refusing to move.

With commendable good humour from the drivers and goodwill from the passengers, and the cooperation of the livestock, we are on our way. The driver sells us the tickets, he obligingly stops at Tsamadou both on the way there and on the way back.

We learn that the buses have been expelled from behind the church for non-payment of rent. Whether they will ever return there, or have to find an alternative location, we will never know, as next morning we are on our way home.

It's our first experience of what to expect of daily life on the islands, and we are completely hooked.

12. Kos – Bubble Beans and Bouzouki

Through a small travel company specialising in slightly off-beat locations, we book a fortnight on Kos island, staying in the quaintly named Drossos Hovel, a simple stone building painted white inside and out and sitting right on the beach.

Despite its name, it is spotlessly clean, with minimal basic furniture and sweeping views across the beach and down to the sea. The nearest building is a temporary beach restaurant a couple of hundred yards away, where they serve the best moussaka, and play taped music by an as yet largely unknown singer, named Chris de Burgh.

This is a perfect family holiday. Outside the front door is a small concrete verandah shaded by a large tree and some creeping grapevines. Silver sands lead to the turquoise waters of the Aegean Sea twenty yards away. The children dash backwards and forwards collecting seashells, splashing in the water and hanging around the restaurant which also sells ice creams and soft drinks. There is so little traffic that it's safe for our sixteen-year-old son to ride a hired scooter to the livelier resort of Kardamena.

The hovel is served by a maid, who arrives each morning with freshly-baked bread, a basket of fruit, a pot of honey and yoghurt, and anything else I have asked for the previous day. Even so, I barely ask for anything as we can walk into Kos town in ten minutes.

It's many years before Kos will become a popular tourist destination. There are no radios on the beach, no olde Englishe tea shoppes. We can walk for hours on the beach without meeting another soul or hearing another human. At night, we sit on the verandah watching geckos hunt for insects on the walls, where the only sounds are the gentle lapping of the waves and the chirruping of crickets.

Our maid's name is Yanni. He is a retired policeman from Crete, a very small, wiry man, brown as a chestnut, with black curly hair and a permanent smile. We quickly become friends, and he invites us to visit his farm. It's a parched, dusty piece of land that yields abundant crops of fruits and vegetables, some planted in the soil and many others growing in old oil cans. There is a big woolly ram pawing and eating its way down a row of watermelons. It comes running up to Yanni bleating and lowering its large head to be scratched.

Yanni tells us that when he bought his little farm there was no water there, and he was told he was wasting his time and money trying to grow anything. However, he believed that he would find water, so hired people to dig wells and drill, without success. As a last resort, he employed a water diviner, who came with his forked stick and walked around for an hour, then pointed to the place where he said there would be water.

Traditionally, when you start searching for water on your land, you buy a lamb which will be sacrificed and roasted if the search is successful, so Yanni bought a young sheep when he began his search.

He and his friends had almost given up digging at the place the water diviner had marked, when a trickle of water appeared.

They sunk a well which yields permanent water, but it is still a precious resource to be used sparingly. Yanni waters his rows of vegetables from a small tin can, giving them no more than a dribble and they seem to be thriving.

'But what about the ram?' we ask.

During the time it had taken to find the water, Yanni had become too fond of it, so he bought meat from the butcher for the celebratory meal, and the animal now lives on the farm, helping itself to whatever it wants.

While we are standing admiring his fruit, a large winged creature bangs into my head, making me jump. He waves it away with his hand, saying 'It's only a bubble bean.' Ever since, whenever I see a bumble bee, I remember Yanni.

We ask him to tell us about his life as a working policeman on Crete.

Had he arrested anybody? Were there any murderers there?

There were no murderers. Crete was a peaceful island and everybody was so happy there they didn't need to kill people. He had never arrested anybody. If he caught somebody doing something wrong, he took them to a café and bought them a coffee. He talked to them and made them promise to behave themselves which they always did thereafter. We must visit Crete – which he calls Kriti – because it is the most beautiful place in the world.

He invites us to join him and his wife for dinner at a small restaurant up in the mountains. It is a beautiful evening of exquisite food (Greek lemon potatoes, who knew such deliciousness existed?) and lively company.

Yanni's wife Xanthipe is a glamorous woman, a modern Aphrodite with wavy auburn hair down to her shoulders, and a cleavage that would make Lollobrigida look flat-chested. Yanni fell in love with her the first time he saw her, and they were married when she was fourteen. It is obvious that forty years later he is still besotted with her. She carries herself with a regal, rather imperious air, and his eyes never leave her. Although she seems friendly and charming, I don't completely warm to her for no reason I can identify. She doesn't speak English so we can only communicate through smiles.

Yanni takes us up into the hills overlooking the Aegean to a small deserted village of old stone cottages. Previously, it was inhabited by farmers who had to take their produce to market on mules down steep, winding paths. They have been relocated to new properties closer to the roads, and the entire village is abandoned.

There are beautiful little homes for sale for just a few hundred pounds. Bubble beans buzz over the wild thyme that fills the air with its scent, while tortoises scramble through the rocks and wild goats jump around on the rooftops.

It's breathtakingly lovely. We are so tempted; we could buy the whole village for the cost of a semi-detached house in southern England. It could be a viable project, in collaboration with some of our friends, for developing into a collection of idyllic holiday homes.

The cost isn't an issue, but the island's proximity to Greece's historical enemy, Turkey, is a problem. Foreigners can only buy land here in partnership with a Greek national. The only Greeks we know are Yanni and Xanthipe, and Xanthipe is very much the dominant partner of their marriage. We will have to form a company with her as the main shareholder.

Although we have lost our hearts to the village, we resist Yanni's urging to buy immediately. It's a huge undertaking and not something we could or would want to do alone. We'll come back next year when we have talked to our friends in England to see if they want to get involved.

On the last evening of our stay, we invite Yanni and Xanthipe to have a meal with us in Kos town. Yanni is very excited about the idea of us buying and renovating the village. Asking when we plan to return, he suggests that rather than booking a package trip, we buy cheap flights and stay with them at their house in Kos town, where they rent out rooms.

It's awkward, because we have been looking forward to the delicious informality of Drossos Hovel, but what do you say when friends make an offer like that? Neither of us has the courage to risk offending them, so we leave with a promise to let them know the date of our arrival the following year.

*****

Yanni is waiting for us when we arrive at the airport on our return to Kos, with a huge smile and his elderly car. He drives us to his large modern single-storey house, where Xanthipe shows us to a spacious, clean room.

Then our holiday from hell begins.

The heat is stifling. The multitudes of mosquitoes are ravenous. The bedroom has a sliding door. If we leave the window open, the mosquitoes keep us awake all night, and the door rattles if there is the slightest breeze. If we close the window, we can't breathe. Behind the house is a field wherein lives a cow and calf. The second day we are there the calf is taken away. The cow moos and cries mournfully, non-stop, day and night. Three houses away is a *bouzouki* bar. It opens at midnight, and *bouzoukies* until daylight. Sleep is impossible.

Another room in the house is rented out to a pleasant Greek lady doctor and her daughter, a girl of about twelve who is learning English. She practises on us. The sliding doors cannot be locked, and she erupts through them unannounced at any time she wishes, shouting:

'Today I am go beach.'

'Today I am go eat.'

'Today I am go swim.'

'Today I am go hot.'

'You want fru-it?'

By the third morning, we are ticking off the days until we can go home.

Breakfast is wonderful. Fresh baked fragrant Greek bread with honey, creamy yoghurt, succulent watermelon, thick sweet Greek coffee and sticky pastries. It is the highlight of our day, before we set off, red-eyed and yawning to try to find a peaceful park or beach where we can sleep for a few hours. We long for the peace of Drossos Hovel far from the noise and disturbance of the town centre.

Every morning, Yanni asks: 'You are having a great time, yes?' And we nod politely but untruthfully.

We return to visit the deserted village. Our friends in England are interested and want to know more. Purchase is a complicated procedure, especially as all the documents are written in Greek and we are dependent on Yanni to explain them. When he has done so we are none the wiser and I don't have the impression he completely understands them either. We will talk again with our friends when we are home and see if we can find out more about how to proceed.

Finally, the blessed day dawns when we are due to fly home.

We ask Yanni how much we owe for our rooms, and he calls Xanthipe – that is her department. She hands us a piece of paper with an astronomical amount written on it. I think she had put too many zeros – maybe Greek numerals are written differently. I cross one off and show it to her. She shakes her head and writes the figure again. The amount would have paid for our air fares and all-inclusive holiday in a five star hotel.

We have put aside the amount that a modest hotel would cost us, but it is less than half Xanthipe's bill. We call Yanni and explain that we don't have sufficient money with us to settle all the bill.

There is a rapid exchange between them, and she is plainly very angry. Yanni tells us that our breakfasts are a gift from Xanthipe. She has only charged us for the room. She is very upset that we can't pay her in full. We promise that we will send the balance when we are home. Xanthipe scowls angrily and walks away.

Yanni drives us to the airport and we part with considerable embarrassment.

We send the balance owing for our fearsomely expensive and dreadful holiday, as well as a gift of crystal wine glasses. We never hear from them again.

As much as we want to return to beautiful, unspoilt Kos, it would be too embarrassing if we were to meet Yanni. The dream of owning a little stone cottage in the hills that smell of thyme remains a dream.

13. Kriti – Rocks and Rain

Disillusioned by our experience in Kos but still in love with Greece, our next destination is Crete.

'Ah, Kriti, it is the most beautiful island in the world,' Yanni had assured us. We decide to find out if that is true.

We book a fortnight at the beginning of September when the weather in Crete will, we are told, be at its best. Our accommodation is in a shared villa in Chania, a short distance from the harbour. The villa is named after El Greco, who had reputedly lived there back in the mists of time.

Chania is a spectacularly pretty town, and El Greco is quaint and comfortable, in a little passage close to the Venetian harbour, and shared with two other couples. The couple in the room immediately below are us are our age, lively and friendly. On the same floor as us is another room, where a woman pops her head out of the door as we are passing, but retreats like a retracting tortoise before we have an opportunity to speak. During the two weeks we are staying there, we never see her again.

The weather is as perfect as we could have hoped, the scenery is romantic, the food is delicious and we enjoy exploring Chania and its restaurants with our new friends.

On our third day, we go to hike the Samaria Gorge, which is to be the highlight of our stay. We leave when it's still dark to start from Omalos, four thousand feet above sea level. It's only ten miles to the end of the gorge, mostly downhill, so we anticipate having ample time to reach the ferry which is the only way back to Chania and which leaves at 5.00 pm.

Ignorance truly is bliss. Because so much of the hike is downhill and the rest is on the level, I have imagined it will be easy, and if we make reasonable time we should reach Agia Roumeli for lunch.

The first part of the hike is down a long steep descent which is punishing on the knees. Our trainers are not ideal footwear. The terrain is rough and rock-strewn. We have to watch every step. You do not want to injure yourself here. There is no means for any vehicle to reach the gorge. Currently, the only way out if you cannot walk is by donkey.

A group of young Germans are seeing how fast they can complete the hike, running and jumping from rock to rock. A sign warns hikers not to shout up at the rocks, as it can cause a rockfall. One of the Germans shouts up at the rocks to test them.

By the time we have reached the half-way point, my feet are agony, have grown three sizes and no longer fit in my trainers, so I have to stamp the backs down, pushing as much of my foot as I can into the front part and trying to hold them on with my toes. I try walking barefoot but that's even worse as the rocks are almost too hot to touch. With no way back the only option is to keep going. We come across little streams and sit soaking our feet to cool them down, before limping onwards. It's very hot. I thought we would be at the end of the gorge by now, but it is still not even in sight. Occasionally, small rocks fall from high above us, dislodging others as they bounce down to the riverbed.

I'm not the only one who is footsore and hot. People around us are hobbling along, with T-shirts wrapped around their heads to protect them from the blazing sun which is now directly overhead.

It's over seven hours since we began walking. I know I can't go much further.

A man trots past and says cheerfully: 'Keep going, you're almost there!'

The so-called Iron Gates stand where the gorge ends at a narrow fissure between the rocks. We can see them now, it's no more than 100 yards. Just as the man said, we really are almost there!

My triumph is short-lived. We have reached the end of the gorge, but I am dismayed to find there are another two miles to walk before we reach Agia Roumeli. If we miss the ferry, there is no accommodation available there and we'll have to spend the night on the beach.

Sometimes you believe you can't do something, but you have to, and you do. And so it was. I tottered onto the ferry and kicked off my trainers. My feet were raw and blistered, the soles throbbing, and when we arrived back in Chania, Terry had to carry me piggy-back to the villa.

When I look back, all I remember seeing that day is rocks: rocks behind us, rocks ahead of us, rocks on each side of us and rocks underfoot.

The following day we hire a scooter. Much as I hate riding on them, my feet and legs are too tired to do much walking. We ride a few miles along the coast and find a deserted beach where we sunbathe in the sand dunes and read. It's blissful.

And then we see a tall figure striding purposefully towards us. It looks as if he's carrying a very long gun. Why would anybody be carrying a gun on a deserted beach, where there is no wildlife? What or who do they plan to shoot? Have we unwittingly strayed onto private property? There's nowhere to run even if I could run, so we stand up and wait for him to approach.

He is like a character who has stepped out of a film. Very thin, extremely tall, wearing a little peaked cap. A tanned and deeply-lined face with black sweeping eyebrows that tilt upwards, and a matching moustache. His nose is rather long and pointed, and under the moustache his mouth is a thin straight line. Black eyes like obsidian. Despite the heat, he is wearing long trousers and a type of quilted jacket. His bare arms are sinewy. He rests his rifle, which looks like something you would find in an antique shop, against one leg and swings a canvas pouch from his shoulder.

He dips his hand into the pouch and pulls out a bunch of fat green grapes, which he hands to Terry. Terry reaches into his pocket and pulls out a handful of coins, but the man closes his hand and pushes it back towards his pocket.

'*Kalispera*', he says as he walks away.

'*Efharisto*' I call after him.

We watch him until he vanishes from sight around a small headland.

71

There is no sign of any habitation in any direction.

The grapes are luscious and juicy and ideal for quenching our thirst on a hot afternoon.

*****

Five days after our arrival, we wake in the night. Water is plopping through the ceiling onto the bed. There's a howling storm, rain lashing down and wind smashing the shutters backwards and forwards against the walls.

In the small bedroom, there is nowhere we can move the bed where the rain will not land on it. We cover it with plastic shopping bags. Sleep is impossible with the noise of the water dripping on the bags. The bed becomes increasingly wet and cold. We go and sit downstairs in the lounge and sleep as best we can.

Bleary-eyed, we share breakfast with our new friends Rich and Helen, who have slept through the night and are surprised to learn there has been a storm. During a brief respite in the downpour, the four of us paddle down to the sea front. The street outside is an ankle-deep, fast-flowing stream.

The sea has climbed out of its bed and taken up residence on the harbour. The restaurants are under water, their awnings ripped to shreds, their chairs and tables overturned. The harbour front is heaped with piles of seaweed and flotsam.

Sploshing into the town centre, we visit a museum and admire shards of pottery with Greek labels which we do not understand. The cinema is showing *Rambo* in Greek. It is bitterly cold and we are all soaked up to our knees.

We find a clothes shop where I buy a sweater. It is hideous, a *Starsky and Hutch* design in thick scratchy wool, but it is warm. Unable to find anywhere selling blankets, we buy a large woolly rug to put on our bed, a sheet of thick plastic to keep the rain off, and several towels to place over the plastic sheet to deaden the sound of the rain hammering on it.

If we want entertainment, we are going to have to make it ourselves. Fortunately, we are all avid readers with a fine supply of books to read in the villa's pleasant lounge.

The villa's hot water system is powered by solar panels. As there is no sun, there is no hot water, and there will not be for the remaining nine days of our stay.

Terry buys two bottles of wine.

Back in El Greco, we settle down in the lounge with mugs of coffee and a plate of biscuits, wrapped in our warmest clothes and reading in companionable silence.

'Did you know,' says a voice from the doorway 'there are at least ten thousand species of spiders in Australia?'

Our neighbour from the first floor, husband of the reclusive wife, appears in the doorway. A portly man, with a long beard.

We all lay down our books and introduce ourselves. We learn that our neighbour is a tax inspector, and a leading member of something called the Evangelist Church of Sweet Running Waters. When we mention that we have friends who own a restaurant in the town where he lives, he says he knows them, as they are being investigated for tax evasion.

He talks at great length about the church. It sounds very jolly. The congregation sing hymns and play tambourines, cymbals and small tinkly bells. We listen politely for half an hour while he talks, and politely decline his invitation to join him for prayers. Moving on from the church, he gives a lengthy monologue on how the tax system had changed over the years.

Rich jumps up, claps his hands and says: 'Who's ready for lunch?' Terry and I jump up too, dashing through the rain and the swirling streams around our ankles until we find one of the few tavernas still open. We're tucked away in the darkest corner when Rich gives a sudden groan.

'Oh, for goodness sake.'

Peering through the rain-lashed window is the tax inspector. He raises his hand and comes over to our table, pulling up a chair.

'I thought I'd lost you,' he says. 'Been looking everywhere. But seek and ye shall find: Matthew 7:7.'

By 8.00 pm we are in bed. I'm wearing the scratchy cardigan because it's so cold, even with the bed covered with the rug.

Terry opens one of the bottles of what he thought was wine. It isn't. It's retsina and tastes of turpentine.

It is the most uncomfortable night with the rug sliding around and the plastic rustling. First thing next morning, we try to find some way of leaving beautiful Kriti. We are too late. There are no more flights for another week. Being pragmatists, we decide to make the best of it.

Despite the cold and the rain, we do enjoy our holiday. Good company, good books and a sense of humour help the time pass pleasantly until our departure.

The tax inspector with the hidden wife is one of those people who is completely insensitive to others. He dominates every conversation with monologues on subjects of his own choosing and which none of us are interested in, so we do our best to avoid him.

Rich and Helen tap on their ceiling with a stick, which tells us they are ready to go out. We creep as quietly as possible down the stairs and out of the front door, then we run as fast as we possibly can, diving down narrow alleys and hiding in shop fronts, with our hands over our mouth to stop the shrieks of laughter. Sometimes we see our persecutor hunting us. The funny thing is that he doesn't realise we are deliberately avoiding him. Every time we do meet him, he welcomes himself with a huge smile and apologises that he missed us.

The sudden devaluation of the Drachma means we can eat at the finest restaurants and enjoy the best wines. The Cretan people we meet during our forays out into the tempest are charming, kind and sympathetic, apologetic for the failure of their climate. It's a different kind of holiday to that which we expected, but it's still quite a lot of fun.

When we arrive in Heraklion for our home-bound flight, it's snowing on the beach.

Would we ever go back again to Crete? A million times yes. Maybe not in September. And maybe somewhere with reliable water heating.

14. Symi – A Taste of Honey

After Samos, Kos and Crete, our next destination is the tiny island of Symi, which gets my vote as the most picturesque of all the Greek islands we have visited.

On the ferry from Rhodes, I am aware of a man with a thick head of long, prematurely silver hair, a silver moustache and the brightest, saddest eyes the colour of chicory flowers. He is staring at me intently, which I find disconcerting. I mention this to Terry, who looks over at him. He stands up and comes over to introduce himself.

His name is Nikolaos, he says, but his friends call him Nick.

He makes friendly conversation all the way to the beautiful harbour and helps heave our luggage up the 500 stone steps to our pretty villa. He says he will call tomorrow morning to check if we need anything. We assume he is connected in some way to the travel agency we have booked through.

True to his word, Nick turns up late morning on a phut-phutting scooter. He has volunteered to be our guide and source of information during our fourteen-day stay. He shows us where to find the best beaches, buy the best bread, cheese, wine, coffee, and which are the best restaurants. He organises a boat trip around the island for us with his friend. There is nothing to pay. He tells us he does not work for the travel agency; he simply likes us and wants us to enjoy Symi.

There's a small shop fifty yards from the villa where we buy our daily breakfasts, and a vine-covered terrace where we sunbathe and read. Julie, at fifteen, is in her element, free to roam around the island on her own. She announces she is going down to the harbour to find a boyfriend, which she successfully does, and spends most of her days with him and a group of friends.

We meet an English couple, a television producer of children's programmes, and his wife, who have a beautiful home on the island, where they invite us for drinks and have an interesting story to tell.

They had been trying to start a family for several years, without success. Because of this, the wife suffered from severe depression, so they had bought a house on the island and moved here hoping that it would help her to recover.

Greek neighbours asked why they had no children. They explained that it was a cause of great sadness for them, but specialists had confirmed that it was not possible for the wife to bear children.

The neighbour brushed that aside. Of course it was possible! All they needed to do was to buy a small golden image of a baby and go to the monastery at Panormitis. There they should light a candle and hang the golden baby with all the dozens of other images and ask St Michael to send them a baby.

At the neighbour's insistence, that is what they did, and nine months later they were blessed with a son. A curious tale, but true.

There is a darker side to Symi, they say. Because of interbreeding on the island, there are many handicapped locals who are kept hidden from view during the tourist season.

On the ferry, we had also met English actor James Windsor. He is understudying Michael Crawford for the lead role in the West End play *Barnum*. He's here for peace and quiet and to learn to ride a unicycle for the part. He has a starring role here, as he practices in a small square, entertaining the crowd who gather there to watch and cheer him on.

You meet the most interesting people in the most unexpected places.

*****

Nick takes us for a picnic to a little cove, where he introduces us to his family. His wife is a large woman with a single angry eyebrow, silent and sullen, with all the warmth and charm of an Easter Island carving. There is a dear little girl of eight who stands with her hand on my shoulder, stroking my hair, and a glowering four-year-old boy.

It's a most uncomfortable afternoon. Nick's wife emanates silent hatred, and the small boy throws stones at me, hitting my ankle bones with painful accuracy and smirking at his mother. Nick spends the whole time sitting on a rock in the sea staring at the horizon, while Terry and I murmur about how lovely the views are and I keep trying to move out of range of the stones. We have no idea why we have been brought here, even less what we have done to upset Nick's wife, and we can't wait to go home.

We are more than dismayed when Nick tells us the following day that he is preparing a very special lamb *stifado* for us (long before we stopped eating meat). The meat has been marinating in a mixture of wine and herbs since yesterday. We are to have dinner at his house this evening, and he won't accept a refusal.

He collects us in his car and takes us to his house. His wife sits at the dining table scowling, and the small boy kicks me under the table. Nick has done all the cooking and does all the serving, while his wife sits, eats nothing and says nothing. We feel like actors in a play who haven't been allowed to read the script.

What have we done to deserve this friendship? Why is Nick so kind to us? The saying 'Beware of Greeks bearing gifts' is still ringing in my ears from our Kos experience. Why are his wife and small boy so openly hostile?

The next day Nick arrives to take us to another of his 'special' beaches, not far from our villa. Terry can walk, he explains, it's only half a mile down a stony track. He insists I must ride with him on his scooter, which I do with extreme reluctance. I fell off one many years ago, in Nairobi, and have never forgotten the humiliation and pain of lying on scorching tarmac, amidst dense traffic, with a red-hot exhaust pipe burning my leg and my mini-skirt up around my armpits. But Nick almost lifts me onto the seat and tells me to put my arms around him, tightly, and trust him.

Terry sets off ahead of us, and after the scooter has bumped and phutted down the track for a couple of hundred yards, Nick stops, turns off the engine and declares that I have sweet blood, and he loves me. He has loved me from the first moment he saw me on the ferry and he has been looking after me in case the *kamaki* get me.

'What is a *kamaki?*' I ask. The *kamaki* are very, very bad men. Only after one thing. '*Kamaki*' means 'trident'. The *kamaki* men wait for the ferry to bring in beautiful English girls like me, they take them and get them drunk, so they can stick their *kamakis* in them. 'A lot of bad diseases,' he said darkly.

I thank him for looking after me, although I point out that Terry is well able to stop anybody sticking their *kamaki* in me if they try to do so.

I'm never very good in these situations, hating to hurt or offend. Trying to make light of the moment, I say we both love him too – he has become a dear friend to us.

No, he replies, he doesn't want to be my friend. He wants me to be his lover. He loves me so much.

'But,' I say, 'we are married to other people. You can't fall in love with somebody you only met a few days ago.'

'You don't love me?' His eyes fill with tears.

'Yes, as a friend, not in any other way. Come on, let's go – Terry will wonder where we are.'

'But you can learn to love me.'

'No, Nick. You are very special. We are friends, but I don't love you any other way, and I never will. We will soon be going home.'

'But you are the same like her. You look like her. Like the woman I really love so much. Too much.' His tears are threatening to overflow from those extraordinarily blue eyes.

'Tell me about her,' I say.

And here is the story of a Greek drama that unfolded ten years earlier.

When he was a merchant seaman, Nick had met a Greek girl in Durban, South Africa. They had fallen in love, and she had come to live with him in Symi. For nearly a year, they had lived in a small cottage overlooking the sea. They ate vegetables they grew themselves, fish they caught themselves, bread, cheese and wine from the friendly owners of the local shops. They were, he said, one soul.

Then they had run out of money, so Nick had to return to sea, leaving his lady in the small cottage. He was gone for eight months, regularly sending money and letters, but never receiving a reply.

When he returned, she had gone. She had left a letter.

In it, she told of how, as soon as he had gone, the local people had turned against her, ostracised her and shouted at her, and the friendly owners of the local shops refused to serve her. 'Go away!' they had told her, 'you don't belong here! Go back to your family. Leave our men alone!'

She had heard nothing from him in all the time he was away. Without news and money, friendless and isolated, she was forced to contact her family in South Africa to ask for help. They sent money for her to buy a ticket to return there.

Nick learned that his mother and sisters had arranged to have all his mail delivered to them so that his letters and the money he sent had never reached the girl. The women of his family had driven away the woman he loved.

He flew to Durban and found out where her family lived. He went there and knocked on the door. Her mother answered the door. She told him her daughter had brought shame upon the family by going to live with him; she was lucky that a decent man had been prepared to accept her. They had married two weeks ago. No, she would not tell him where they lived. She closed the door.

Poor Nick, as he tells me this, the tears are running down his cheeks.

When he returned to Symi, his mother would give him no peace until he married a local girl. After they were married, his wife had opened the chest where he kept all the mementos and souvenirs of his travels around the world, the whole history of his life in the navy. Carvings and postcards, seashells and stones, ethnic goods — small things worth nothing in terms of money, but for him irreplaceable treasures. And one photo of his lost love.

His wife burned everything while he was out, and left a pile of ash on the steps. He has never forgiven her, and he doesn't love her. She is jealous and resentful of other women and the son is under his mother's influence, rude and disobedient. There is no possibility for divorce.

'One day, I will go back to South Africa and find her,' he says.

'We need to go, Nick,' I say gently. 'Terry will be worried. Come on.'

'Please put your arms around me again,' he says, as I reluctantly climb back onto the scooter. I lean my head against his back and wrap my arms round his chest.

Silently, we ride down to the beach to join Terry, eat ice cream and toss pebbles into the water.

Nick mentions that during the tourist season there are many people kept locked away by their families, because they are 'not normal' and would frighten visitors, confirming what our English friends had told us.

'Because Symi people must always marry other Symi people,' he says, bitterly. 'No people from other places. So now too many people with things wrong with them.'

As beautiful as the island is, with the scent of herbs, coffee, fresh-baked bread and moussaka, with the blue waters of the Aegean sparkling in the sun, the simmering emotion begins to feel oppressive.

On our last evening, we invite Nick to join us for dinner, to thank him for all his kindness. We have ordered lobster – or as it is written on the menu, 'lombster'.

The lombsters are succulent, the wine is delicious, there is Greek dancing and plate smashing. Nick is very quiet. We say our final farewell and wave as he zig-zags away on his scooter, back to his house, to the wife he doesn't love, his pretty little daughter and the stone-throwing boy.

Next morning, our ferry is late leaving. The captain is pacing around on the harbour, looking around as if he is expecting somebody. We are standing on deck for a last look at beautiful Symi, when we hear shouting, hooting and the phut-phutting of a speeding scooter.

Nick is racing along the sea wall. He jumps from his scooter, speaks to the ferry captain, then runs up the gangway carrying a large can and waving to us.

'Honey!' he shouts. He tells us he collected it in a plastic bowl this morning from his friend, whose bees feast on the wild thyme that smothers the island. Then he took it to another friend's factory to have it canned so that we could carry it safely. The friend had phoned the harbour to tell the ferry captain not to sail until Nick arrived.

'Best Symi honey, so you will remember Nick, and Symi.' he says. He presses a piece of paper into my palm and walks back down onto the dock, turning once to wave as the ferry pulls away.

I read the piece of paper. On it, he has written his address, and 'Please write to me. I love you.'

For a few moments, I imagine having a romantic, platonic friendship with this lonely, handsome man who has held up a ferry to bring me a gift.

I hold the paper in my hand until Symi is out of sight, and then I let it fly into the air and twirl into the sea.

Whenever I see or taste honey scented with thyme, I think of Nick and wonder if he ever did go and find the lady he had loved and lost. I'd like to think he did.

15. Brief Encounter

When I was five years old, my mother used to walk with me to the end of our road and put me on a bus to go to school. We were the only residents in our road who owned a motor vehicle, my father's motorcycle and side car, but it was only for occasional weekend outings. Everywhere we went was by public transport.

We lived in South West London, and my early memories are of grey pavements and grey houses edged by small privet hedges, and mostly grey skies. There were very few vehicles on the road so the arrival of the red double-decker bus was a welcome sight, bringing a burst of colour into our lives. My mother would hand me up onto the platform, and the conductor would lead me to a seat, before reaching up and pulling twice on the cord that rang the bell to tell the driver everybody was aboard. I would hand over the fare, and the conductor would punch out a ticket from a metal ticket machine dangling from a leather strap around his neck. I held on to the metal handle of the seat in front, until the bus pulled in to the bus station, where I had to change to another bus for the final leg of the journey. That bus stopped near the entrance to the convent school which I reluctantly attended. After school, I took the two-bus return journey and my mother would be waiting at the bus stop to walk me the short distance home.

It was perfectly normal in those days. Families walked if they were near enough, otherwise they put the children onto public transport. We lived three miles away, too far to walk. With so little traffic on the roads, and having been indoctrinated to always look right, left and right again before crossing, road traffic accidents were very rare.

I enjoyed the bus ride a great deal more than I enjoyed the school.

One of my classmates travelled to and from school by train, and when one day she invited me to go home with her for tea, I eagerly accepted. I was blasé about bus rides, but had never been on a train so the idea was incredibly exciting. As soon as the bell went to signal it was time to go home, with our satchels on our backs we walked the short distance to the train station.

How I managed to get on that train I have no idea. I wouldn't have had a ticket (unless I'd managed to steal some other child's or children's money from their desks – a story from my childhood memoir, *I Wish I Could Say I Was Sorry*).

It was quite a step for little legs from the platform to the carriage, but there was somebody there to help us up. It wasn't so much the noise of the engine, the heavy clunking of the doors, the hissing of the steam (yes, this was before the line was electrified), the metallic smell, the lurching as the train moved off, the screeching of the whistle nor the clacking of the wheels on the track that thrilled me, and it wasn't even knowing perfectly well that I was doing something naughty for which there would be consequences. What they would be (what my mother would think when I didn't arrive) I had no idea.

I felt a massive kick of excitement and expectation, one I still have today whenever I board a train. I believe that was the moment my passion for travel was born.

(In case you are wondering the outcome of this early adventure, my little friend's mother was surprised at her unannounced guest, gave us a hurried tea and took me home via train and bus to the relief of my frantic mother. No telephones in those days!).

There is something about a railway station that reeks of adventure and the unknown. People anxiously studying timetables, checking tickets, running along dragging luggage as the doors begin to close, waving, crying, shouting. I could happily spend an entire day sitting at a busy station watching the activity.

However many train journeys I've taken since then, I still get that same buzz when I step aboard, whether it's a few stops or hundreds of miles.

For romance, the Mombasa to Nairobi line wins. I vividly remember our first trip from the port of Mombasa to the city of Nairobi, when we arrived in Kenya in 1954. Three hundred miles chugging gently through the African night, eating in the dining car at a table laid with a crisp white tablecloth, with a small table lamp on each table, and china plates. Swaying gently down the corridor back to the compartment which had been converted, during the dining time, into cosy bunks with linen sheets and green woollen blankets.

Leaving the palms and banana groves of the coast and climbing slowly uphill until daybreak revealed vast herds of animals grazing upon the plains – zebra, giraffe, wildebeest, gazelles. Arrival at the noisy, colourful, smelly station in Nairobi where porters with handcarts battled each other for the privilege of carrying our luggage. Magic.

There's a new express train now which completes the journey in less than five hours instead of the twelve hours it once took. That holds no appeal for me. I want to see and soak up the scenery, not watch it flash past in a blur.

But it doesn't have to be romantic or long distance; I simply love climbing on any train, wondering what will happen, who I'll meet.

It's mid-morning and I'm taking a train from St Albans to London. There is only one other person on the platform, a middle-aged man who is marching on the spot and swinging his arms. I avoid looking at him because he makes me feel uncomfortable.

When the train pulls into the station, I climb into the nearest carriage, which is empty. I'm disconcerted when the marching man gets into the same carriage and sits opposite me. I pull out my book and pretend to be reading, wondering how I shall defend myself if he attacks. There's no emergency cord to pull. I decide that if he makes a move towards me, I will knee him as hard as I can between his legs. I've done it once before and know how effective it is as a deterrent.

'Excuse me, are you going to London?' he asks.

I look up into a gentle, smiling face.

'Yes,' I reply. 'Are you?'

'No, I am going back to Shenley,' he says.

(There is a progressive mental hospital at Shenley, where patients are at liberty to come and go as they wish.)

'Do you work in London?' he asks.

'Yes, I do.'

'Do you know my brother? He works in London.'

'What does your brother do, and where does he work?' I ask.

'Well, he's an accountant, but I don't know where he works. Maybe he works where you work.'

He takes out from his jacket pocket a little plastic wallet and fishes out a business card which he hands to me.

'If you see him, please will you ask him why he didn't come last week. He comes to see me every Saturday, but this time he didn't come. I don't know why'. He looked so downcast. I say that there are so many people in London that I may not see his brother, but if I do I will be sure to pass on his message.

That satisfies him and he puts away the card.

'Are you happy at Shenley?' I ask. 'Do you like living there?'

'Oh yes, it's very nice. We do lots of activities and make things. We have open days when you can come and see all the things we make.'

He hesitates, then says: 'The only thing I don't like so much is the food. It's not very good really. Sometimes it isn't cooked enough, and sometimes it's burnt.'

'Oh dear,' I reply.

'What's the food like where you are?' he asks.

'Pretty much the same.' I reply quite truthfully. I haven't yet mastered cooking.

He nods in sympathy.

As the train slows down for his station, he stands up and stretches out his hand.

'Goodbye, it's been very nice meeting you. Take care. See you soon,' he says.

I shake his hand, he steps down onto the platform and waves as the train pulls away.

16. 3.40 am

I'm returning from England, due to arrive in the early evening in Poitiers, where Terry will be waiting.

The ferry crossing is on time. The chuggy little train from Dieppe to Rouen is on time. There is a comfortable change over time at Rouen, enough to allow me to enjoy a coffee and stroll around admiring the Art Nouveau station.

The train to Paris leaves on time. So far everything is going according to plan. I settle down for the 90-minute journey and close my eyes.

Fifteen minutes from Rouen, the train squeals and comes to an unscheduled halt just outside a station.

Nobody reacts at first, reading or chatting quietly. But as time ticks away it is evident something is amiss. The engine of the train has been switched off. Passengers have become restless, murmuring and peering out of the windows.

I feel anxious because I don't have a great deal of time to get across Paris to catch my train to Poitiers. After another ten minutes has passed, I know I'll miss my connection.

A voice over the speaker announces that somebody has jumped onto the line in front of the train and been killed. The judicial police have arrived on the scene (ugh, how awful for them), and we will not be moving again until they have completed their examination.

In England, the announcement would be of 'an incident on the line'. Of course, everybody would understand the implication, but the graphic words wouldn't be spoken. The French are less coquettish, more down to earth.

The announcement continues to say that those making a connection in Paris should speak to the official who will be coming into the carriage to make arrangements for those whose journey will be disrupted.

A friendly French couple sitting opposite me tell me how lucky I am – as I'll miss the last train home, the SNCF will have to put me up in a hotel in Paris for the night. Woo hoo. It seems wrong, somebody has just died, but who wouldn't appreciate an all-expenses paid night in the City of Light?

The ticket man gives me a voucher to present at St Lazare, and I am already anticipating a nice cosy hotel room and dinner, hopefully breakfast too, all thanks to the efficient and thoughtful SNCF.

It is a long time before we begin rolling again and when we arrive at St Lazare station, it's pandemonium, as several hundred delayed people with vouchers storm the *Accueil*. When I eventually reach the counter to claim my hotel room, I am disappointed to learn that the SNCF have made alternative arrangements.

The Paris to Biarritz overnight train will make an unscheduled stop at Poitiers for my benefit. I try to feel grateful.

I am told to take the Métro to the Gare d'Austerlitz to catch the train from there. I explain that I don't use underground trains or lifts because I'm claustrophobic. The official shrugs and suggests I take a taxi.

There seems to be no end to the queue for taxis, so it is fortunate that my train doesn't leave for another three hours. I tack myself to the end of the queue and shuffle along as it diminishes. It is snowing gently. Despite the cold and the long wait, everybody is good-humoured and patient. I generally find the French are in these situations. I am quite enjoying listening to their banter, until I remember I only have seven Euros in cash with me. How will I pay the taxi driver?

Finally at the head of the queue, I have an inspiration. I turn around and call out in French to the crowd behind me: 'Does anybody want to share a taxi to Gare d'Austerlitz?'

People stare in astonishment, as if I've taken off all my clothes and am rolling naked in the snow singing Hallelujah. For a few seconds there is silence, then from the far end of the queue a man holds up his arm and yells 'Yes!'

He gallops up and we climb into the taxi together.

He has very little time to make his connection to somewhere far away in Eastern France. He doesn't think he'll make it, but at least now he has a chance. He asks the taxi driver to put his foot down, which leads to an enjoyably high-speed, sightseeing tour through Paris, like something out of a film, as the driver points out landmarks that pass in a smudge.

When we approach the station, I take out my purse with the seven Euros in it, but my fellow passenger waves it aside, leaps out, thrusts a bundle of notes at the driver and vanishes.

'Ooof, he's overpaid me!' says the driver. Yay! Result.

I was due in Poitiers at 7.00 pm. Terry will, I know, be waiting and wondering what has happened. He doesn't have a mobile phone. It is now after 10.00 pm. I find a phone box and call home, but there is no answer. I leave a message to say I am OK and don't know what time I'll reach Poitiers.

The washrooms at the station are immaculate, warm, sparkling clean and with showers, so I enjoy a thorough freshen up and then roam around the station, and blow the seven Euros on a hot chocolate and croissant.

At a quarter to midnight, I present my voucher to a harassed French official who is doing his best dealing with a dozen people all asking questions and shouting. I find my allocated seat and snuggle down as the Biarritz train moves out of the station. The passenger in front of me has thick, luxuriant black hair and is playing a Walkman. He immediately reclines his seat into my lap. Through his earphones, the *tchk tchk tchk* noise goes around and around. His hair needs washing. I jerk my knees into the back of his seat a few times to try and disturb him, to no avail. I go and stand in the area between the carriages and watch the night going by.

There is nothing to see. Not a light anywhere. No road traffic. Just empty blackness. After two hours, a small alarm bell goes off in my head. Surely by now there should be some signs of habitation? Either I am on the wrong train, or they have forgotten to stop. Maybe I have totally misunderstood and the train is actually heading non-stop to Biarritz. How will I get back home? I wish I hadn't spent the seven Euros.

The carriages are dark, everybody is asleep. On and on rolls the train as I stand there swaying and wondering if the person who had jumped in front of the train near Rouen had given a thought to how many people would find their day disrupted, let alone the distress of all those who had to deal with the aftermath of their actions.

Beneath the tiredness and anxiety there is, I admit, just a tiny tingle of excitement wondering how this is going to end. Bizarrely, the words of one of Chris de Burgh's songs keeps running through my head: something about a man wasting my time by being on the line.

Finally, the train begins to slow, and as it pulls up I read the station sign for Poitiers.

It's like a scene from a wartime spy film: a deserted station, a silent train, a single passenger alighting, a solitary figure standing on the platform beneath a single faint overhead light. It is 3.40 am. Terry has been waiting here since 7.00 pm.

As he takes my backpack, a carriage door slams. A figure descends and follows us out of the station.

'Excuse me,' he says in French.'I am sorry to ask, but do you go anywhere near Roches Prémarie. He lives alone, there is nobody he can call for a lift, and at this time of night in Poitiers, there are no taxis nor hotels open.

Happily, we pass right past his front door on our way home. We are even able to offer him a swig of brandy from a flask Terry has thoughtfully brought with him.

That is what I love so much about train travel – you just never know what may happen.

17. The Bordello

We are driving through France on our way down to Spain to holiday with friends at their villa. Our two children have gone ahead with the others while we are following more sedately.

We're an hour or so from the ferry when we run into a violent storm on the motorway. The wipers can't keep up and we can barely see through the windscreen. We pull off at the next exit, planning to sit there and wait for the rain to subside.

Immediately we drive through the exit we see it's a mistake. There's no way back onto the motorway. We try to reverse through the barrier without success and we can't see any sign to indicate where we are. We wait until the rain slackens off and follow the road through the land that time seems to have forgotten. There is no traffic on the road, and no sign of any habitation. Darkness falls and we decide we'll have to find somewhere to stop for the night, before starting off again next morning when we know where we are and how to get back to the motorway.

Through two small towns we go. Not a glimmer of light from anywhere. Everywhere is closed. We're discussing the possibility of pulling onto the side of the road and sleeping in the car, when we enter a small village. We spot a light on in a café and behold! An illuminated sign in the window reads 'Chambres'.

An elderly woman is piling chairs onto the tables and pushing a grubby mop around the floor. I ask if it's too late for coffee, and yes, she replies, it is. Does she have a room for us?

'For how long?' she asks.

'Just for one night, please.'

We have to pay in advance.

She goes behind a counter and takes a key from a hook, then beckons us to follow her up the stairs. As we near the top, a man comes bouncing down, winks at us and makes a clicking noise with his tongue as he passes. I have no idea why, but I smile at him.

Madame stops outside a door and points down a dingy corridor. 'The toilet is down there,' she says.

Well, I hadn't expected an *en suite*. As long as there is a clean bed, we'll be happy.

She hands the key to Terry and goes back downstairs.

The first thing I notice about the room is that there is no wardrobe, no drawers, nowhere to put our clothes. Not that it matters as we will only be there overnight, but still. There is just a bed, and a bidet.

It's a knocking shop. However, our choices are limited to either making the best of it here, or sitting in the car for the rest of the night.

Terry goes down to the car and collects all our beach towels. We spread them carefully over the top of the bed and lie down upon them, fully clothed, and manage a few hours of fitful sleep.

As soon as daylight arrives, we scoop up the towels and stuff them in the boot of the car. We choose not to investigate the toilet, but hold on until we reach somewhere more salubrious.

Unlike the many luxury hotels which I seldom remember much about, I won't forget the night we spent in a bordello.

18. Skiing – Italy: Building Rockets

On one of the perpetually grey English winter afternoons, we have lunched with friends and are watching *Ski Sunday* on the television. The glistening snow and blue, cloudless sky contrast with the grey murk and rain slapping against the window. A lithe, tanned figure swooshes down the slopes with effortless ease. Effortless. Just standing there on skis and almost flying.

'Why don't we go skiing?' says a voice. My voice.

Two months later, we're disembarking at foggy Milan airport, en route to our ski resort which, until a year ago, had been a potato-growing area in the Lombardy region of Italy. We are my best friend Gina, her husband Jack who has taken control of the venture, Terry and myself.

Jack is not only my best friend's husband, he's also one of my husband's best friends, and his boss. He's generally good-natured, loud and larger than life. He's also the ultimate control freak as we quickly discover.

The fight to reclaim our luggage looks like turning nasty when a couple of Hooray Henrys shoulder their skis and swing around, smashing Jack on the side of his head. Gina restrains him as he prepares to take a swing.

'Oh, ya, frightfully sorry,' says one of the Henrys, swinging in the opposite direction and almost catching him on the other side of his head.

The luggage piled onto the conveyor topples off into the central area. Somebody starts to clamber over the conveyor. An angry Italian man in a uniform elbows his way through the crowd and shouts at the clamberer. The clamberer shouts back, pointing at the tangled heap of skis and bags. The angry Italian joins him and the two of them reload the belt.

Once we have retrieved our luggage, we haul it through the thrashing maelstrom of humanity to our coach, which is belching out clouds of toxic smoke. The driver is hurling bags into the hold. He tries to snatch Gina's holdall, but she hangs on tenaciously. It's Hermès and cost several thousand pounds.

'*Darmi la borsa, per favore, Signora*,' he says.

'You're not putting my wife's bag in with that lot,' says Jack. 'Forget it, Sunshine.'

There's a bruise coming up on his face.

The driver shrugs, and we climb into the coach. The seats are narrow, the aisle is narrow and Gina's holdall bangs into seated passengers as we pass.

We sit waiting for the remaining passengers to arrive. The driver is drumming his fingers impatiently on the steering wheel, and our tour guide is hanging from the open door, scanning the crowds.

A moving mountain of luggage comes into view, pushed by a very small man with a little boy walking beside him. Behind him slinks a tall woman wearing furs and dark glasses, and another tall woman, not wearing furs and dark glasses, carrying a baby. The very small man has a beard that curls upwards and is wearing a bobble hat, which gives him the appearance of a gnome. He is dwarfed by the luggage trolley, which threatens to topple its gigantic burden as he weaves through the crowd.

Arriving at the coach, the two women climb aboard and settle themselves comfortably. Outside, the small man begins to unload the trolley and pack its contents into the hold, while the small boy watches. The fur/dark glasses woman lights a cigarette and exhales a languid stream of smoke onto the head of the passenger in front of her. Her companion jigs the baby up and down and they talk loudly in a language I don't recognise. After rearranging all the luggage several times in order to fit it all in, the small man and little boy find two remaining seats in the coach, and we're off.

The journey to the resort takes twice as long as it should because fog limits visibility to about twenty feet. By the time we reach our destination it's 2.15 am. The coach stops on a road a hundred yards outside the town.

'Everybody,' calls the rep, clapping her hands. 'This is as far as the coach can go. We'll just walk a couple of minutes to the centre and I'll take you to your hotels.'

The first passenger jumps down from the coach and falls down, hard. 'Watch out!' he shouts. 'It's lethal.'

The road is thick ice, I mean ice several inches deep. Rock hard. In our thin-soled, stiletto-heeled boots, Gina and I grope our way to the luggage hold and wait for the driver to drag out our bags.

'I can't walk on this,' I say.

'You'll have to, Sweetie.' says Jack. 'Otherwise you're in for a long cold night.'

Terry tucks his arm under mine, gripping me firmly, and together we drag our bags along the road by the light of the coach headlights. People are slipping, sliding and falling over all around, like skittles. Conversation is limited to expletives.

Ahead of us in the foggy gloom, the diminutive gnome-like man is carrying the small boy and towing a sledge piled with the baggage and skis. The fur coat woman and her companion, wearing sensible après-ski footwear, are carrying nothing. The sledge swings from side to side. The bags fall off. Still holding the child, the little man tries to reload the sledge. Jack and Terry help him while the women stand by, chatting.

We slither into the sleeping village. A church bell tolls mournfully.

The rep claps her hands and calls out: 'All those staying at *Casa Bella*, can you come over here, please?'

Several people shuffle forward and the rep bangs heartily on a hotel door which is opened by a weary looking man. He and the rep mutter to each other, and the shufflers disappear behind the door.

We work our way through the village, dropping off groups at various hotels. By the street lights, we can see right through the ice down to the pavements inches below. What I notice is that there isn't a single snowflake to be seen anywhere.

Our hotel is the very last one, illuminated by a faint sign that says

'*Albergo*' at the top of a slight upward incline which is like a toboggan run. Even in their shoes the men are having difficulty not sliding backwards. In our high heels Gina and I simply can't make the climb, so our husbands go ahead and deposit the luggage at the door, then come back down to tow us up.

It must look funny but it's a miracle we all reach the door of the *albergo* without injury.

The hotel is dark and silent. The door is locked, and there is no bell, so the rep knocks, and then knocks again, while we try to retain our footing on the icy surface in the freezing night air.

We are not dressed to stand around in sub-zero temperatures, at night, in the mountains. As hypothermia begins to get a grip, the door opens a crack, and a woman in a dressing gown peers out. She doesn't seem to be expecting people to arrive in the early hours of the morning, but with much sighing and many *porca miserias* she lets us in and hands out room keys, muttering about passports and police. We haven't eaten since a light snack on the plane, and I ask if there is any food available.

'*Sì, sì,*' she replies. '*Domani.*'

She walks away, leaving us standing in the chilly corridor.

'What did she say?' asks Jack.

'She says we can eat tomorrow.'

Our rooms are small, clean, and bitterly cold. The internal walls seem to be constructed of cardboard reinforced with striped wallpaper, and the *en-suite* bathroom comprises a teeny washbasin, a strange lavatory with a shelf halfway down the inside, and a shower cubicle with a plastic curtain. Our washbasin tap is dripping, and no force is powerful enough to stop it.

We wrap ourselves in duvets while we eat our evening meal – a packet of mint toffees found in my pocket, that we share out and wash down with tap water drunk from a plastic cup on the washbasin shelf.

We slide into the icy bed and shiver ourselves to sleep.

'Hands off cocks and on with socks!' roars Jack. 'Let's be having you lazy buggers. It's seven o'clock,' he continues. 'We're waiting in the dining room.'

We've had four hours sleep.

Terry springs up in the pitch darkness of our room, banging his knee on the bedside table.

'Where's the light?' he asks.

'I don't know. I can't see anything.'

Feeling his way around the walls, he arrives at the window, pushing it open and thrusting the shutters back. Light streams in. Grey, damp light revealing the full extent of our skiing paradise. Glistening icy slopes pierced by stunted trees, and rocks. The shower is cold, but there's tepid water in the basin, adequate for what my grandmother used to refer to as 'a lick and a promise'.

We follow the smell of coffee to a room that looks like a hospital cafeteria. Formica tables and hard plastic chairs with tubular legs. The tables are set with a typical Italian breakfast: small coffee cups and a plastic basket containing some packets of biscuits and pastries. A young girl fills the cups with thick black coffee.

Jack points to the plastic basket. 'I'm not eating cakes for breakfast.' he says. 'Go and talk to the woman and ask her to organise a cooked breakfast.'

'They don't eat cooked breakfast in Italy,' I say.

'Tell her that English people do and ask her to cook something for us.'

Signora is sitting behind the makeshift reception desk, reading a newspaper.

'*Buon giorno,*' I say hesitantly.

'*Buon giorno, Signora,*' she replies.

'What can I do for you?'

'We were wondering,' I say, 'if it would be possible to have a cooked breakfast.'

'Cooked breakfast?' she frowns. 'What do you mean, "cooked breakfast?"'

I explain that in England, we usually have a hot meal at breakfast time, but she purses her lips and replies that we are in Italy, where breakfast is not cooked.

'Well, do you think we could have some eggs? We are all very hungry, because we didn't have anything to eat last night.'

'*Bene*,' she mutters. 'Eggs.'

Ten minutes later, she arrives with a tray bearing four boiled eggs rolling about on a plate, and a jug of excellent coffee.

'*Uove*,' she says, pointing at the eggs.

'Bread?' I ask.

'No,' she says, pointing at the tray of cakes. '*Dolci*.'

Jack points at the coffee and says in a very loud voice: 'TEA.'

'*Caffè*,' she replies and walks away.

Swanking our fashionable salopettes and matching jackets we set off for the ski shop. The road is perilously icy. Even in our après-ski boots we slither and slide. There is not a flake of snow.

A gruff man fits us all out with skis and boots.

The boots are excruciatingly uncomfortable, too loose for my feet and too tight on my ankles. They come halfway up my shins and are secured with metal clips that have already broken one of my fingernails. My skis are three feet taller than I am. There are poles to manage too, dangling around my wrists. The boots crank my legs forwards so I walk like something out of *Aliens*. We shuffle our way to the slope to await our instructor, who is booked for 10.00 am.

With time to spare, Terry is eager to get started so he says he'll give me a quick lesson. He has skied once before, about twenty-five years earlier, for half an hour on a small hill in Wales.

I think I look pretty good in my ski goggles, cream ski-suit and fake-fur hat, although the bent-kneed posture caused by the boots somewhat spoils the effect.

Terry has put his skis on and is carrying mine over his shoulder, while holding onto my elbow to pull me over the ice to the children's drag lift, which is a series of black plastic handles at hip level, attached to a moving steel cable heading uphill.

I snap the uncomfortable boots into the unfeasibly long skis.

Terry says: 'Grab a handle when it comes past.'

A black handle goes by. I snatch at it, missing the first one, lunge for the next one and fall forward onto my face, the skis slipping behind me. After being dragged for a few yards. I let go of the handle and slide back on my stomach to where Terry is standing.

He heaves me back up onto the skis, and next time, I snatch firmly on the handle and begin to glide gracefully up the hill. At the top, I see the cable turns around a concrete pillar and goes back downhill.

'Let go now!' Terry bellows. That's definitely what to do, otherwise I'll be dragged around the pillar and returned to the bottom. So I let go of the handle and immediately slide backwards, crash into Terry who is following on the next handle, and knock us both to the ground, along with several children behind us.

Terry gets to his feet and pulls me onto the piste, a wide sheet of ice.

'Up you get,' he says.

With difficulty, no longer feeling elegant, I untangle my feet and stand upright. The skis start sliding backwards down the slope. Terry grabs one of the poles dangling from my wrist and brings me to a halt.

'Now, we're just going to ski very slowly down here.' he says. 'It's easy, just follow me and do what I do.'

Letting go of me, he turns downhill. Clumsily, I turn around too.

And I'm skiing! Yes, in the swanky cream-coloured ski-suit, goggles and fake-fur hat, I am actually skiing on the ice, picking up speed, overtaking Terry and heading at Mach 1 straight towards the stone wall of the hotel. Wow!

'Plough!' Terry yells. 'Plough!'

'Help!' I scream back. 'I can't stop!'

'Turn your toes in!' he roars.

I point my toes together. The wall is approaching terrifyingly quickly. The skis have gathered speed and there is an inevitability that I'm going to be wiped out, like a cartoon character going through the wall and leaving a me-shaped hole. I put my gloved hands over my face to protect my teeth from the impact. I can see in my mind the scarlet mess I will make when I hit the wall.

Then something that feels like a train smashes into my right side. I briefly find myself airborne before thumping onto the ice with one leg behind me, still attached to the ski, and a shooting pain in my ankle, lying on my back looking up at the blue sky and a laughing face.

'You nearly had it then! I saved your life,' laughs Jack. 'You shouldn't try to ski before you know how to stop.'

I roll onto my side six feet from the wall.

'Come on, let's get you up and at it again,' says Jack, yanking me to my feet.

'Only way to learn. Straight back onto it, like falling off a horse. By the time you've had your hundredth fall, you'll be a class A skier.'

Terry arrives, looking slightly sheepish. 'You should have ploughed,' he says.

'If I knew what it meant, I would have done!' I glare.

All around, people are tumbling over and shrieking. It's nothing at all like *Ski Sunday*. Especially with no snow.

Jack tugs me towards the black handle and I manage to make an identical exhibition of myself to the one I did five minutes earlier. Tiny, tiny children, barely up to my knees, are swooping confidently around on the slopes, making me feel completely inadequate as I slither helplessly over the ice and Jack knocks me down again. I'm not sure I'm going to enjoy skiing.

The instructor is standing a short distance away, beckoning us over. Gina arrives, magnificent in a scarlet outfit, matching lipstick, designer glasses and a small white blob of sunscreen on her nose. I notice that she is managing to walk quite confidently in her boots and is carrying her own skis. She is gorgeous, glamorous, warm, generous, feisty and funny. I love her to bits.

Winded from the falls I've taken on the ice, I decide to sit for a while to get my breath and dignity back. Assuring them that I am fine and will join them shortly, I watch them tramp over to the instructor, followed by the little gnome in a woolly bobble hat.

Gripping onto the wall of the hotel, I grope my way back to the hut and hand in my skis, then plop down on a chair on the hotel's patio. I unclip the locks on the boots and slip my feet out, putting them up on another chair. Our group are listening earnestly to the instructor, and stepping sideways up a small slope. The gnome is having trouble, he keeps slipping back down.

Terry breaks away from the group lesson to come and urge me to join them. I point at my ankle, which is starting to swell, and say I'm more than happy to sit and watch this morning. I'll see how I feel later.

Within an hour, the group have moved higher up the mountain, except for the gnome man who has taken off his skis and trudged disconsolately back to a nearby hotel, where the two women are sunbathing on a balcony and the little boy is sitting on a chair swinging his legs back and forth.

At noon, my three companions are back, beaming and laughing and congratulating each other on their achievements. Gina has never skied before, but she's a natural and fearless athlete and has found her feet immediately. Terry too is completely fearless, and Jack is showing off as he skies down the icy slope, legs wide apart, arms in the air, like a four-legged, jet-propelled starfish, and swooshing to a halt inches in front of us.

We find lunch in a small, noisy and blissfully warm restaurant. It's the first time we've all felt really warm since we left Milan. Fuelled by a plate of polenta served with a rich sauce and lashings of Parmesan cheese, washed down with several glasses of *vin brulé*, I feel there's nothing I can't do, until I stand up and my ankle crumples.

I'm ready to give skiing another try, but my swollen foot won't go into the ski boot, so I am cheerfully consigned back to the chair in the sunshine, and that's the end of my first day as a would-be skier.

When the other three return as the sun begins to go down, they are buzzing with excitement, and promise that tomorrow they'll help me to catch up with them. I ask what happened to the gnome.

'We kicked him off,' says Jack. 'He couldn't keep up with us.'

Back in the chilly hotel, we wash as best we can in the tepid water and meet downstairs for dinner, which comes in the form of a heap of *tagliatelle* followed by pork cutlets. It's adequate but not very exciting. There is no lounge in the hotel, so we walk the short distance to see what entertainment the town has to offer.

This is the town's first season since it transitioned from a potato farm to a ski resort so it's quite limited, but we find a cosy bar where we sit in front of a log fire and sample the liqueurs on offer. I become addicted to Sambuca topped with roasted coffee beans and set on fire.

We discuss my failure to make any progress skiing, and agree that the baby slope is too short to give me time to get the hang of the plough. Tomorrow, we'll go higher up to where there is more room. To pluck up courage to return to our cold rooms, we drink rather more than we should. In this fuzzy glow, we assure each other that everything will be better tomorrow.

Jack wakes us early again. The skies are still grey, with mist hanging on the mountains, and we have headaches.

In the ski hut, we stamp into our boots. I have strapped my swollen foot with a crepe bandage, and manage to slide it into my boot. There has still been no snowfall, and we are walking on thick sheet ice.

This morning, we will concentrate on finding a way of making me stop and turn so that I can catch up with the others.

Terry hauls me by one of the ski poles until we reach the bottom of the button lift.

'This is far easier than the handle,' says Gina encouragingly. 'You just grab the pole as it goes by, stick the little round seat between your legs, and let it drag you up. I'll stay behind you, so don't worry if you fall.' As there is no snow, the button lift buttons don't come down as low as they should and you need to give a little jump to mount them. I miss a couple, but manage to capture the next one, wobbling up to a level part on the mountain where Terry and Jack are waiting. Riding behind me, Gina scoops me up as I dismount from the button, and stops me from sliding back into the following person. I feel utterly helpless and hopeless.

'Right, Sweetie,' Jack says. 'We're going to get you back down.' He points to a long slope.

'We'll warm you up with a gentle downhill run,' he continues. 'Then we'll get you up on a red run once we've taught you how to plough.'

He demonstrates the snow plough, toes pointed in, inner edge of skis cutting into the ice.

Gina adds, helpfully: 'And squat. Push your bum back as if you were straining to go to the loo.'

The piste does look beguiling and gentle and I'm pretty sure I can manage this, so I turn and face downhill.

Immediately, the skis take on a life of their own and slide over the ice. For a few glorious seconds, I am skiing down the slope, starting to gather speed. I point my toes together, squat and stick my backside out as far as it will go to put Gina's advice into practice. It has no effect. I try to put the brakes on by poking the ski poles into the ice, but they just skid along the surface.

My leg joints and back don't bend in the way they should since I cracked my spine and pelvis when I was fourteen. I was given false expectations watching *Ski Sunday*. It is not as easy as it looks, not as effortless. It didn't show how bendy you need to be to make the skis do what you want them to, and particularly how to stop them.

Still, I've watched enough quadriplegic people and even blind people skiing to know that anything can be overcome with determination, and I do want to be a good skier, gliding and swooping through the snow, if we ever have any.

'EDGE! EDGE! Uses your EDGES!' barks Jack. The ski edges will not gouge into the ice; either they are not sufficiently sharp, or I'm not sticking my backside out far enough, because they don't find any grip. While the three of them tack easily from side to side on the slope, I head steadfastly downhill gathering speed by the yard, despite being pigeon-toed and sticking my backside out. Shortly before impact with a cluster of trees, Jack brings me to a halt by skiing into me and knocking me over. In that manner, we return to the bottom of the mountain, where the instructor is waiting.

I wave the fearless three off, and sit happily in the weak sun, boots off, with a glass of *vin brulé*. Ah, that's better.

The little man is still on the baby slope, still side-stepping up the hill a few yards, and then turning to ski downwards. He seems to have mastered the snow plough, and can stop at will. I'm envious.

One of the women shouts to him in a foreign language, and he tramps over to where they are sitting. After a brief conversation, he snaps off his skis and takes the little boy by his hand into the hotel. They emerge a few minutes later with an ice cream, then the little man settles the boy back on his chair and returns to the slopes. The two women appear to be asleep.

Several times during the morning, he is summoned to attend either to the boy, or to a baby crying in the buggy.

At lunchtime, we go up on a button lift to a chalet serving delicious hot polenta with blue cheese. My three friends are bubbling over with excitement – they're already on black runs. They're going to learn parallel turns this afternoon. The instructor says they're the quickest learners he's ever had.

They're concerned that they have abandoned me, but I insist, quite truthfully, that for this afternoon, I am more than happy to sit and watch, then tomorrow I'll have another try.

By the time they return from their afternoon instruction, it has become very cold. A deep hot bath would be perfect, but there is no bath, and neither is the water really hot. However, the shower tray is quite deep, so we fill a plastic bag with water and use it as a plug to block the outlet, then fill the tray with the tepid water and take it in turns to curl up in it in a foetal position. It isn't very satisfactory.

After dinner – *tagliatelle* and pork cutlets, the same as last night – maybe it's the Signora's signature dish, we head into town again. We find a bar where a local man befriends us and asks if we have heard about the

Italian space exploration programme, and would we like to see an Italian rocket.

First, we must all order a glass of Amaretto, the almond-flavoured Italian liqueur which is delicious, like drinking liquid marzipan, served with the crunchy little *amaretti* biscuits individually wrapped in a kind of tissue paper.

Our new friend carefully collects all the wrappers and smooths them out. 'Now,' he says, 'this is how we build a rocket.'

He rolls a wrapper around his finger to form a cylinder, which he stands upright on a plate.

Then he touches a match to the top edge. 'This is lift-off!' he say as the rocket floats upwards for a couple of feet before falling back to the table in a heap of ash.

It's rather entertaining, and we order several more glasses of Amaretto and *amaretti* so we can practice building and launching Italian rockets.

When we get back to the hotel, Signora is still up and about, so we broach the subject of heating and hot water. She brushes aside our complaints, saying that it's winter, we cannot expect it to feel tropical.

Over breakfast (boiled eggs and cakes), I suggest that while the others continue with their instruction, I keep practising on my own as I think it will work better for all of us. I won't feel so stressed and they won't be wasting time.

On my own and with no pressure, I make a little progress. At least I can manage the lifts and find a way to bring myself to a halt. It isn't elegant, but it works. There's a relatively gentle slope where I start to get the feel of the skis, and can snowplough and turn, clumsily, but still, I can do it. I've become a skier! I'm relieved to know I'm not the complete numpty I thought I was.

When the other three return for lunch, they are pleased to see me in action at last, as if between us we have achieved a miracle. We ski back down to the hut for lunch and celebrate my success, as if I've won an Olympic gold medal. Jack says I'm ready to move on to the next stage.

After lunch, we take a chair lift up to a higher and much steeper slope, whereupon Jack takes over my training. It's a matter of honour that he should succeed in making me a competent skier. As I crash, skid and tumble, there are guffaws of laughter from him, while I'm a mess of despair, pain, seething rage and humiliation. I really don't think I want to spend another skiing holiday with Jack.

At least the air is fresh and dry, the sky deepest blue, the landscape beautiful beneath its shiny coat of ice and, of course, the food is exquisite.

On day four, a group of Americans arrive at the hotel. Suddenly, miraculously the radiators spring to life and the shower pumps out scalding water. Breakfast has undergone a change too. Next morning, there's a choice of hot chocolate and a wide selection of fancy pastries as well as cold meats, cheeses and two types of bread.

By the end of the week, three of our party have progressed to parallel turns, skiing black runs and jumping moguls, while I can ski down a gentle slope and stop at the bottom.

Unlike the others, I have not received a certificate, nor a little badge to wear, testifying I am an experienced skier who has conquered the black runs. However, I've read four books, eaten my fill of the best of northern Italy's cuisine, and can build and launch a rocket made from a biscuit wrapper. Although it hadn't started well, it has been fun, mostly.

After breakfast on the final day, as we wait for the coach to take us back to Milan, the first snowflakes begin to fall.

19. Skiing – Germany – Setting the House on Fire

The following year, we drive to Germany in Jack's Aston Martin. Gina and I crush into the back of the car, knees jammed into our chins, and we set the Autobahn on fire. This machine has a top speed of 190 mph, and Jack enjoys demonstrating his driving skills, pushing it to the limit. He's pleasantly relaxed now, because he's in full control and he speaks German.

Gina only had a baby two months ago, but she's back to her tiny, slender pre-baby weight and fighting fit.

We arrive at our pretty, cosy guest house on the edge of a forest in a popular ski resort in Bavaria. The snow is deep and crisp, the branches of the trees bowing beneath its weight.

Several other couples drive down to join us, mutual friends, most of whom can ski proficiently, and I'm pleased to know that one of the wives is as good a skier as I am.

'Right, you lot,' says Jack, as we all prepare to turn in for the night. 'Breakfast at 8.00 am and we leave for the slopes at 9.00 sharp. Anybody not ready gets left behind.'

Breakfast here is a feast. There are dishes of cold meats, platters heaped with a variety of cheeses, home-baked breads, jams and honey.

On the pistes, the snow is thick and firm, and it's a great deal to easier to snowplough than it was on ice. I may never be a skier able to manage steep runs, or do parallel turns, but now I can enjoy leisurely runs in company with Judy, the other novice skier. She and I are left to do our own thing, while Jack is busy organising the other members of the party.

While we are lunching one day, a young American comes over and introduces himself. He's a snowboarder who lives locally, and he invites

Jack, Terry, Gina and myself to watch some videos he thinks we'll enjoy. He draws a map of where he lives, and we arrange to see him there that evening.

After dinner, we set off in the Aston Martin. The route leads into a very dark part of the forest. There is no sign of any human life for miles, and the further we drive, the more uncomfortable we become. It's not often you see Jack or Terry feeling anxious, but we begin to wonder if it's sensible to be going somewhere to meet somebody we don't know, so far from civilisation. Has our host seen the car and assumed we are horribly rich? Does he plan to hold us to ransom, or kill us and steal the car? Nobody else knows where we are going. We debate turning around or, if we go on, how to deal with an attack.

When we finally reach the 'house,' it appears to be a deserted military barracks. There is no light showing. The men go in first, leaving Gina and I in the car with the engine running and instructions on what to do if they don't return soon.

We wait anxiously in the dark, until a door opens. Light streams out. Terry signals us into a large, sparsely-furnished room with just a few chairs. The walls are covered with animals' heads and weapons – ancient maces, axes, chains, swords, crossbows, flails, pikes, giant hammers and guns with fixed bayonets. It's reminiscent of a scene from a horror movie, just waiting for the host to come out with a machine gun and spray us.

Instead, he appears with a tray of beers and some smoked cheese, and explains that the building is used by the American military for training exercises.

We watch some videos of snowboarding and extreme skiing. All the time I can't help expecting something awful to happen; masked men will come storming through the door and lock us in a cellar, or maybe our host is a lone operator, and the beer and cheese are drugged, and we'll become unconscious, or die, so he can strip us of all our jewellery, expensive watches, Gina's sable coat, and steal the car. It doesn't seem plausible that a complete stranger would invite us to this isolated place just to show us some videos. I'm watching for any signs of lethargy, or suspicious movements, thinking that if anything does kick off, I will try to grab the mace and chain off the wall and beat our attackers to death. I get quite lost in a reverie, imagining twirling the weapon around, creating mayhem, saving us all from a horrible fate and redeeming myself for not being much of a skier.

As it turns out there is no need to prepare for battle, because all that happens is that we watch a load of videos, drink a couple of beers and eat some cheese. I'm almost disappointed after mentally practising my moves with the mace and chain.

Our stay passes very pleasantly as the proficient skiers spend the days racing each other, while Judy and I continue our leisurely activities on the lower slopes.

Just when I am feeling confident on my skis, we all drive to another resort for the day. There's a queue waiting for the lift. As Judy and I shuffle forwards chatting, I am not paying attention to what is happening ahead. From nowhere, a suspended chair sweeps me off my feet and I find myself dangling on the edge, pulled forward by the weight of my skis, and hanging over a bottomless ravine.

Behind me, Terry shouts: 'Pull the bar down! The bar behind you!'

I twist my neck around as far as it will go. I can see there is a bar at the back of the chair but to pull it down means letting go of my clutch on the frame of the chair, thus risking being pulled off into the abyss by the weight of the skis. Instead, I cling on with all my strength until the chair reaches a plateau where the lift turns around a pillar to descend, then I let go and jump off. The chair continues on its way, thumping me in the back of the neck and knocking me over in a jumble of skis and ski poles.

The snow is knee-deep, sparkly, reflecting the vivid blue of the sky. There's a button lift going up to the next level. While Jack organises races over moguls and overhangs, Judy and I spend the afternoon gliding serenely up and down.

The rest of the group ski back down at the end of the afternoon, leaving Judy and I to take the lift. Going back down on the chair is as freaky as going up, because I still can't pull the bar down in front of me and feel an invisible force dragging me off the seat. As the lift nears the bottom, where it winds around a huge concrete pillar before starting its ascent, I begin to shout to the men standing there.

'Help!'

I don't know how to say it in German, but they obviously understand because as the chairs draw level with them, one of them grabs my arms and swings me clear, and the chair continues on its way.

I really don't understand why everybody else can manage to get to grips with these contraptions in a day, whereas it's taken me almost two weeks and I'm still rubbish.

On the last day, Terry and I go with our friend David to the longest gentle run in the area, over two miles long and smooth. I will definitely be able to do this.

Luckily, the lift to the top has a double chair, so Terry rides with me and pulls down the safety bar. As we climb into the chair, the lift attendant hands each of us a square of canvas to wrap over ourselves, because as the lift climbs we are soon in icy air, which is flecked with tiny golden speckles that float around us. Then a thick grey blanket of fog descends. It's so dense we can barely see each other. The lift climbs silently and there is no way of knowing when we are reaching the top.

Eventually, we see a dim light and hear voices shouting. Arms reach out, grab onto the chair, flip the bar up and swing us out onto a plateau.

Visibility is no more than ten feet. Planting me firmly and telling me not to move until they call me, Terry stations himself a little way down on one side of the piste, and our friend David the other. We are now going to descend, with me skiing from one to the other, and if I can't stop, they will catch me.

And that's how we do it. It's the best skiing I've ever done. The snow is deep and firm, I can zigzag back and forth from the red jacket to the yellow jacket, and it's so exciting, barely able to see anything apart from those coloured jackets. By the time we reach the bottom, I am ready to do it all again, but it's almost dark and the lift has shut down. Just as I have finally managed to ski more than fifty yards and thoroughly enjoyed it.

It's our last night in Bavaria, and Terry is keeping me awake because he is snoring very loudly. I'm a creature who needs lots of undisturbed sleep if I'm not to become a raging monster. Having failed to turn him over and stop the noise, I decamp.

Downstairs in the dining room is a comfortable leather couch. I decide to go and sleep on that. Beside it is a large oak coffee table decorated with a wreath of dried leaves and seeds surrounding a candle.

I take a couple of blankets and install myself on the couch. After a few minutes, I begin to worry that if the lady who sets the breakfast early in the morning comes in and sees a body lying on the couch, she may panic, so I decide to light the candle to give her advance warning.

Having done so, I turn my back and go to sleep.

I'm woken by a rhythmic dripping sound and lie for a while wondering where it could be coming from. Not through the ceiling, that is certain, as there are two floors above the dining room and I can't feel any damp on my blankets. Possibly thawing icicles, but they would not be thawing during the bitter cold of the night. There is no sink nearby that would have a dripping tap.

I try to ignore it and go back to sleep, but the dripping continues in a most annoying way, so I turn over on the couch and come face to face with a wall of flame leaping about on the coffee table.

The candle has melted down and set fire to the seed pods in the wreath, which have jumped onto the table, igniting the table runner which has in turn set fire to the table itself. The melted candle wax is dripping into the remains of the wreath.

I'm aghast. The surface of the table is black and smouldering. The table runner is melted. I mash out the flames with my shoe and retreat to my bedroom until daylight. In the morning, I bang on Jack and Gina's door, and ask Jack to explain to our host and hostess why their coffee table is in ruins.

They are most gracious and refuse any payment towards its renovation, but I'm not at all sure they understood then, or would ever understand, why I had set their table on fire.

20. Skiing – Bulgaria

Terry and I decide to go skiing in Bulgaria because we think it will be interesting to visit a country that has, until two years previously, been a part of the Soviet bloc. Plus, it's cheap.

Arriving at Sofia airport courtesy of Aeroflot, we walk into a riot. Several hundred people have been waiting over two hours for their luggage to appear, and there is nothing happening. Nothing at all. The baggage conveyor is stationary. We join the crowds of frustrated travellers who are shouting at each other, and at everybody in general.

I go to find a loo. Outside the cubicles sits a very, very old wrinkled lady holding out her hand. I put a £1 coin in it, and in return she hands me one sheet of rough toilet paper. Just a single sheet. It seems very expensive. During our stay, we will learn that every public toilet works on the same basis. Toilet paper is expensive and heavily rationed. Our first experience of what life had been like in a communist country.

Back at the riot, Terry has found our tour operator smoking quietly just outside the doors to the terminal, and asks what is happening, or rather not happening.

He learns that the baggage handlers are on strike because they haven't been paid and will not be delivering any luggage until they are, which is unlikely to be in the foreseeable future. The guide seems resigned and not particularly concerned. He says there is nothing he can do about it.

Terry approaches the people who are on the same tour as us, and invites them to contribute to a collection to pay the baggage handlers. One or two people volunteer, the rest prefer not to.

With the equivalent of a few pounds in his hand, Terry climbs down the stationary conveyor into the depths of the terminal, where the baggage handlers sit smoking and chatting. One of them understands a little English and says that if Terry can point out which of the numerous planes lined up on the terminal is ours, they will unload it. It is fortunate that Terry is so passionate about flying and aircraft because he has memorised the registration letters of our plane, and leads them to it.

Half an hour later, the conveyor belt jerks into life and we are able to retrieve our luggage. Other groups of travellers watch enviously.

We seat ourselves on an ancient coach and settle down for the four-hour drive to our resort. By the time we arrive, our eyes are red and swollen from the smoke of our fellow passengers, and we reek of stale beer, also courtesy of our fellow passengers. Bulgaria, we realise too late, isn't just a cheap ski resort. It's also a haven for youths seeking cheap beer and cigarettes.

Our hotel is a fairly spartan concrete building, although it boasts a large, almost Olympic-sized, swimming pool in the cold, gloomy basement. The rooms are small, neat and clean. There is a telephone. It is made from bright orange plastic with an ultra-curly cable, and resembles a child's toy. If the lights are turned on in the bathroom the water does not run. If the water runs, the lights go out.

For breakfast next morning, there is a choice of an apple or half a grapefruit each, and some excellent bread.

A coach waits to take us to the ski slope, a twenty-minute drive away. It fills up with very drunken young men carrying bottles of beer and packets of cigarettes. By the time we arrive at the slopes, our eyes and throats are burning from the cigarette smoke. Once there, we discover that there are no pistes really suitable for novices like myself. It is steep and quite rocky terrain, but luckily there is a cosy chalet that serves hot chocolate, alcoholic drinks and hot snacks, with a wide terrace to sit on and watch the action. The sky is very blue and the sun is very warm, and Terry is very happy skiing. I am more than happy to sit and read and watch the skiers.

We have been told to be ready for the coach to take us back to the hotel at 4.00 pm, and we are not looking forward to the experience. As we make our way to the car park, a tall, handsome man comes over and asks in English if we would like a taxi. His taxi is a vintage and beautifully kept Mercedes with leather seats and a sign that says 'No smoking'. Perfect.

He drives with rather frightening panache, and after dropping us off says that he will wait for us next morning, and not to worry about the fare, we can pay him later.

Each morning, he is waiting as promised outside the hotel, keeping the taxi doors locked so that nobody else can use him. He tells us that he is the Bulgarian rally driving champion, and now runs a school training young rally drivers. Each day we try to pay him and he refuses. We are slightly anxious that we are going to be presented with a huge bill before we leave, but he is so amiable, and to avoid the stench on the coach, we will be happy to pay quite handsomely.

We have a walk around the small town where we are staying and look in the shop windows. There is almost nothing to see. A couple of shapeless brown dresses, some thick nylon stockings, clumpy shoes. It's all rather sad to see how little they have even now.

Two things that they do have in abundance are alcohol and cigarettes. Wine is 10p a bottle, champagne £1. Beer is cheap as chips, as are the cigarettes, but if you want to buy orange juice or chocolate you need to take out a mortgage. Paying in Dollars costs 75% less than paying in Bulgarians *levs*, and small change comes in the form of boiled sweets. At the hotel, the food is really very poor. I notice that the meat is mostly fat and gristle, the parts that in England would be cut off. People grumble and complain. I feel embarrassed for the waiters, who are polite and can't do anything about the quality of the food. We are getting the best that the hotel can provide and no doubt for many years people would have considered themselves lucky to be eating it.

Our tour guide arranges a meal for us at a riverside restaurant. We are met at the front door by a man serving pieces of warm bread sprinkled with cumin. The place is packed and lively, the people are friendly and many of them speak English. We eat freshly-caught trout, deep fried in lard which we try not to think about, and some fried potatoes. We drink local red wine that is ridiculously cheap and extremely good.

Terry has made friends with a local Bulgarian man and they ski together every day. His friend has a flask of brandy made by his grandfather before the Russian Revolution, which they share on the chair lift.

The hotel puts on a rather good cabaret, with very enthusiastic dancing in extravagant costumes, and a lively band that plays 1960s pop songs. I feel humbled by how our hosts are trying to make our stay enjoyable. Tourism is going to become an important part of their economy and help them to improve their quality of life.

With two nights left before we return, we ask our friendly taxi driver if there is a restaurant nearby where we can get a really good meal. He says he'll book a table for us as nobody at the restaurant speaks English, and he will drive us there, which he does. If we call him when we're ready to go back to the hotel, he'll come and collect us.

Although neither of us are fussy eaters and will normally eat anything apart from meat without complaint, the food at our hotel has been virtually inedible and we have been living mainly on bread and chocolate bars.

Our taxi driver hands us into the care of a young waiter with black curly hair, laughing eyes and wearing a collarless white shirt with a red embroidered bolero.

The restaurant is a glorious wooden building, four storeys high. Each floor is divided into small rooms brightly decorated with seating for six to eight people. The waiter leads us to the second floor, into a pine-panelled room decorated with colourful fabrics and paintings. It appears more Turkish than European, a reminder that until 100 years ago Bulgaria had been a part of the Ottoman Empire.

Two stocky dark-haired men in black leather coats are seated at one table. A third man in a black leather coat appears to be fast asleep at another table. The first two black leather-coated men get up and leave immediately. The waiter pulls the third man off his chair so he slumps to the floor then drags him out of the door.

After carefully wiping down a table and pulling out the chairs for us, the waiter disappears for a few moments before returning, then with a flourish, presenting us each with a plasticised menu twelve inches high and folded like a concertina. We search through pages in Italian, French, Spanish, German, Russian, English, Greek, Polish and Dutch. We are almost salivating at the prospect of food as we know it, and we take our time choosing.

We both opt for the *truite au bleu* and point to that when the waiter returns to take our order. He smiles and nods his head, and points to pork.

We shake our heads, and smile, pointing to the trout. Again, he nods and points to pork.

I point to Terry and myself, and make an oinking noise, shaking my head vigorously and saying very loudly 'NO'.

Then I moo, and shake my head vigorously.

I do the same with baa, quack and cockadoodleoo, each time shaking my head and saying loud 'NOs' to indicate that we do not eat meat or poultry.

The waiter joins in, making animal noises and laughing.

I point at trout and make swimming motions with my hands and blow imaginary bubbles, smile, make my eyes big, and nod hard.

He nods too, and points at pork.

Finally, we understand that the only dish available is pork. With much pointing and murmuring, he explains that the multi-language menu is purely for translation purposes. Whatever your language, you point to what you want, and he looks up the Bulgarian equivalent. However, tonight there is only pork.

Later, I learn that in Bulgaria shaking your head means yes, and nodding means no. Little wonder it was so confusing.

We pull sad faces and resign ourselves to going hungry, but he holds up his hand, laughs and skips out of the room. When he returns he brings two plates of beautiful grilled vegetables and some fried potatoes – the best meal we've had during our stay.

When it's time to leave, we say 'taxi' to the waiter expecting him to call our friendly driver. He hops out of the door, holding up his hand to indicate we should wait, which we do.

Ten minutes later, he waves us to follow him down the stairs and out to the deserted street. A large Mercedes pulls up. Out climbs a man who bows to us and hugs the waiter. The waiter strips off his bolero and hands it to the man, then ushers us into the car.

He climbs into the driving seat and drives away smoothly, depositing us back at our hotel, where he absolutely refuses to accept any payment.

As we find so often, it is the people who have the least who are the most generous.

On the final afternoon of our stay, we thank our taxi driver and ask him how much we owe, explaining that we will be leaving the following day for Sofia to catch our flight.

The bill amounts to almost nothing, and half of that if paid in precious dollars.

He asks if we want him to take us to Sofia, a journey of about 90 miles which will cost the equivalent of $12. The roads are rather basic, the journey from the airport had taken nearly 4 hours and neither of us is looking forward to the return trip enveloped in clouds of alcohol and smoke, so we leap at his offer.

At horrible o'clock, the taxi is there waiting. The driver has brought a flask of thick black coffee laced with some kind of fire water to kick us into gear. As the early morning light rises, we pass a rather desolate landscape of tiny farms mostly made up of small fields, fruit trees and higgledy-piggledy houses. We reach a motorway service station, a long modern building with many shop windows, all of which are empty and do not look as if they have ever been open. The coffee shop is brightly lit, all stainless steel, long glass counters and seating for about sixty people.

On the wall, there are pictures of pastries and hot chocolate. We decide to have a cake with our coffee, but when we order it, we are told that there aren't any. Nor is there any hot chocolate, nor milk, nor sugar.

Nothing except coffee.

We drive on into the centre of Sofia, through streets with little traffic and few people. Most of the people are wearing drab, unfashionable clothing and the shop windows display nothing that appeals.

Our driver takes us to visit the monumental St. Alexander Nevsky Cathedral. It is a truly stunning building, both inside and out, and was built to honour the Eastern Russian soldiers killed during the Russian/Turkish War in the late 19th century, which resulted in the liberation of Bulgaria from Turkish rule.

I am not a lover of religious architecture, but Alexander Nevsky Orthodox Christian Cathedral takes your breath away with its size and splendour. It's impressive enough from the outside, neo-Byzantine architecture with domes of brilliant gold and gentle copper green, but the interior is dazzling. It floods your senses with its extravagance and magnificence. Marble, alabaster, vast chandeliers, gold icons, murals, frescoes, mosaics of precious stones, stained glass windows.

There could not be a greater contrast between the opulence of this building and the austerity outside.

When I glance at my watch, I am alarmed to notice that our plane is due to take off in less than an hour. I ask the driver how far it is to the airport, and he asks if we want to visit there. I say yes, we have to catch our plane back to England, and he looks surprised.

'You return home today?'

Yes, that is why we have come to Sofia.

He thought that we just wanted to have a tour of the capital, and for that he has been willing to get up at horrible o'clock, drive for four hours, show us around and drive back for another four hours.

He seems genuinely sad that we are leaving. When I show him our tickets and he sees the departure time, he ushers us swiftly to his car and shows why he is the rally driving champion of Bulgaria as he shoots, races, bumps, corners on two wheels and finally pulls up ten minutes later in a cloud of smoke from the tyres, at the airport terminal. We grab our luggage. Acting as a human bulldozer, the driver sweeps us through the airport to the check-in desk where we have minutes left before the lane closes. After a few words between the driver and the check-in official who snatches our bags and hurls them into a void behind him, we are rushed through before we have a chance to thank him properly, with just enough time to hand him the fare for the taxi, all our remaining change and a $20 note, which he tries to push back into Terry's hand. We wave goodbye, and gallop along a corridor, onto the tarmac and up into Aeroflot, trusting the luggage handlers are back to work and will have time to load our bags.

And so we say Благодаря и довиждане to Bulgaria. It has been an interesting experience and a sometimes frustrating one. We take with us memories of the kindness of the people and an appreciation of how fortunate we are to live in a modern and prosperous country.

21. Italy Again – Dangling in the Air

The following Christmas we decide to go back to Italy where, whatever else may happen, we are assured of the best food. The resort of Bormio, according to the brochure, has plenty of easy runs that will suit Julie and myself, as well as some long and demanding runs for Terry. The Alpine World Skiing Championships were held there last year.

After flying into Milan, we get separated on the coach. Julie and Terry are seated together, and I find myself sitting next to a very, very wide lady wearing an enormous multi-coloured crocheted woolly hat. She takes up most of the available space so I am squashed against the window.

'Me name's Jaminy,' she says, taking my hand and shaking it, 'and me aunty just died.'

'And me cousin got two broken legs.'

'Oh dear.'

'Me brother got took with a real bad virus and now he's blind.'

'Your family really is having a bad time.' I say, shifting as far away as I can on the coach seat.

'Me younger sister had two miscarriages, and me older sister's husband run off and left her with five children.'

'Do you have any relatives who aren't ill?'

'No. Me mam has a collapsed lung and …'

'Oh look,' I squeal, pointing out of the coach window. 'A mountain!'

'I don't think she'll get well, you know,' continues Jaminy. 'She's lost the will.'

'It must be very hard for you all,' I said.

'Jesus cares for us,' she says. 'We put our trust in him and he guides us. We know he has a reason for everything.'

Without warning, she tips sideways and a vast elbow like a bolster whacks into the side of my head as she burrows into a pocket in her jacket. After a struggle, she pulls out a brown book filled with religious tracts and hands it to me.

'There. Choose one you like, and we'll read it together.'

I stare at my reflection in the window. Why, I think, why do I always seem to attract odd people? Why am I sitting next to a giant woman, a total stranger whose family is decaying even as we travel, and who wants me to read from a religious pamphlet?

I know I'm weak and often end up doing things I don't particularly want to do because I don't like offending people by saying no. However, as we have a long drive ahead and I can visualise that the next thing, we'll end up holding hands and singing Kumbaya, I take a deep breath and say:

'No, thank you. Really. I wish you well, but I don't want to read with you.'

She does not seem offended, nor deterred.

'Don't worry then, I'll read to you. This is a good one – from Corinthians.' She enfolds my hand in a podgy paw, and bellows:

Therefore we do not lose heart. Though outwardly we are wasting away, yet inwardly we are being renewed day by day. For our light and momentary troubles are achieving for us an eternal glory that far outweighs them all. So we fix our eyes not on what is seen, but on what is unseen. For what is seen is temporary, but what is unseen is eternal.'

'I think I'll close my eyes and have a little nap,' I say, tugging my hand away and turning my face to the window. I breathe in a deep and meaningful way to indicate that I'm already asleep.

It's impossible to actually sleep with Jaminy's weight crushing me against the side of the coach as she mumbles:

'One thing have I asked of the Lord, that will I seek after: that I may dwell in the house of the Lord all the days of my life, to gaze upon the beauty of the Lord and to inquire in his temple. For he will hide me in his shelter in the day of trouble; he will conceal me under the cover of his tent; he will lift me high upon a rock.'

122

Gosh, Jaminy, I think, I'd be tempted to push you off a rock if I had the opportunity. She reads on for a while, then folds the piece of paper and feeds it back into the envelope, back into her jacket pocket, almost knocking my head through the window with her elbow. I think she has given up but no, she has taken out another pamphlet and is reading from that. I ask her very nicely if she could turn the volume down as it is preventing me from sleeping. And so she does, reading in a sibilant whisper that is even more irritating.

When we reach Bormio, my spirits soar. It is a beautiful old town and the snow is knee-deep. All the buildings are decorated for Christmas, four days away. In the glow of the street lights, it is magical, like fairyland.

After Jaminy has unwedged herself from her seat and forced herself through the door of the coach, we queue up to reclaim our bags and our rep directs us to our accommodation. I am relieved to see that Jaminy is not staying where we are, but give her a little wave as she plods away dragging a suitcase behind her. I feel rather sorry for her. I cannot imagine her on skis.

We have been allocated a spacious apartment in a small private hotel. Not only are there two double beds, there are also easy chairs and a small sofa as well as an *en suite* bathroom with a bath. It's warm and homely, and there is a delicious aroma of freshly-ground coffee wafting from the kitchen.

Bormio is where we find skiing heaven. Everything is perfect. The apartment, the food, the weather, the atmosphere, and most of all the pistes.

We're surprised that there are not that many people in Bormio because it's the perfect place to be for Christmas, with carol singers and roasted chestnuts, sensational decorations and an outdoor ice-skating rink. Heavy snow falls each night. The skies are so blue, the sun so warm, it really is perfection. Terry spends much of the day up on the high slopes while I glide around on the gentler pistes, and Julie divides her time between us. In the deep snow, I can stop at will. Whilst I can't parallel turn – every time I try, I end up crossing my skis – I manage to somewhat clumsily change tack.

Terry and I only ski together on the lower, easy slopes where he soon gets bored, so we go to the tourist office and collect a detailed map showing all the pistes. There's a blue one right from 3,000 metres at the top of the mountain down to the town. Blue runs are easy. I can do those.

Up we go in the gondola, emerging at the top into a wooden cabin which leads out onto an icy wooden platform and slippery steps.

A strip of red and white plastic tape held up by a couple of flimsy spikes marks the very edge of the mountain. It is no more than two yards away down a slight incline which seems to magnetically draw me towards it. On the other side of the tape, there is nothing but fresh air for thousands of feet.

Terry tugs me away to the narrow gulley of ice through which only one person at a time can pass to reach the piste. It is the iciest, slipperiest ice I've ever seen. I cannot get any grip with my ski boots, and flounder around trying not to fall flat on my back. I inch my way along, prodding at the walls of the gulley with my ski poles. It takes so long to negotiate the ten yards that a new gondola full of skiers has arrived and they are caught in the bottleneck behind me, hissing and cursing until we break out onto a plateau.

Far below, the town looks like a child's toy, speckled with tiny ant-like figures. The snow glistens with silver specks and it feels as if we are standing on top of the world. I'm eager to set off and ski all the way from the top to the bottom. We walk along the plateau searching for the start of the blue run. Deciding that it must be a little further down the slope, we head downwards. Suddenly, it's like skiing on a wall. The plateau drops away.

Terry shouts 'Sit down!' which I do, with a thump. I dig my heels and hands as deep as I can into the snow to stop from going any further.

A slinky Italian lady skis towards us and asks if we have a problem. I explain we are trying to find the blue run, but she laughs and says we are on the black run. It's very easy, we should just follow her. She vanishes over the precipice.

The gondola cabin is uphill 100 yards behind us, and only accessible via the icy gulley. The only way is down, and we both know that if I stand up, I won't be able to stop until I hit the bottom.

Happily, a snowplough passes nearby, so we call out to him.

'Is there a blue run here?'

'*Si, signora.*'

'Where is it?'

He waves his arm vaguely. 'It isn't open yet. It opens on New Year's Day.'

That's tomorrow.

He goes on his way.

I'm getting cold sitting in the snow and my bottom feels wet.

'OK,' says Terry, 'this is what we'll do. I will side slip a few yards, and you will let yourself slide forward into my skis. That is how we'll get back down. BUT do not go off track, because if you start to slide past me, I won't be able to stop you. You'll end up rolling down the mountain like a log.'

That's what we do. With my skis on his shoulder, he slips sideways, and then calls me to let go. I lift my heels out of the snow and slide down until I crash into his skis. We repeat this until we reach the chair lift station at Bormio 2,000.

I stand up and limp towards the lift operator, so that he'll think I'm injured and not just pathetic, and he says I can catch one of the chairs going down. He stops the lift. I don't know if anybody has ever taken the lift back down, but the chair is far too high off the ground to be able to climb into, so he has to build a platform out of snow. It takes about ten minutes before it's firm enough and high enough for me to get on. All this time, the passengers coming up from the bottom have been dangling angrily up in the air.

Once I'm aboard, the lift starts again and I enjoy a stately ride to the bottom, while the upcoming passengers stare in astonishment to see anybody going downhill by lift. Terry skis on down hoping for a last run, but by the time he arrives, the lift is closing for the night. We agree we won't try that run again.

With plenty of ski lifts, we have never so far had to queue and the pistes are clear, but that changes on New Year's Day, when we wake up to a shock. Bormio is absolutely teeming with Milanese who have left the city and come to celebrate the first day of the year.

Getting to the lifts has become a battle. It's the law of the jungle, the survival of the fittest, bedlam. The pistes are crowded and you need the agility of an eel to ski without bumping into somebody.

With a week of peaceful skiing behind us, we are philosophical. They only have the weekend to enjoy and we still have a couple of days of skiing left. We wait patiently until everybody else has climbed into the gondolas or hooked onto the lifts.

When the next gondola arrives, we are just about to step into it when we lose out to some nifty foot and elbow work from a group of Italians who squeeze in ahead of us. The gondola is filled to capacity, so we decide to wait a while and have a coffee.

While we're sitting out in the sun, we hear some excited noise and see a crowd of people pointing up to where the gondola is hanging, unmoving, about thirty yards above the snow. The passengers are striking at the windows and shouting, while below them officials are standing around chatting and laughing, showing little sense of urgency.

Eventually a gondola descends from a parallel cable and stops alongside its crippled colleague. It is not, as we imagined, bringing engineers to release the stuck gondola and allow it to continue its journey. Nope – the marooned people have to step out and across the void into the other gondola. We can hear their screams as they are helped to safety, and both gondolas begin to sway. I can imagine their terror and am supremely grateful to those people who were so anxious to get ahead of us, because I am certain that in their situation I would have (a) suffered from claustrophobia and (b) fallen between the two gondolas.

One day, I'd love to return to Bormio for Christmas.

22. Andorra

Every year, when one ski holiday ends, I say: 'That's the last time.' Yet somehow every year, we're packing our gear and heading for the slippery slopes. Each time I vow that I will conquer parallel turns and red runs, and each time I return home after varying degrees of failure. What would be ideal for me is a resort with nothing but long, gentle runs. Terry, however, wants to ski the steepest slopes, so we try to find somewhere that suits us both.

This time it's a budget holiday in Andorra over the Christmas and New Year period.

We fly into Toulouse, transferring from there by coach to the hotel in Andorra la Vella. Our coach driver stops every half hour and disappears, and it's 3.00 am when we arrive. Unlike the cosy rooms featured on the hotel's brochure, ours is spartan, with a sagging bed so that we both roll into the middle, like sharing a hammock. It's quite impossible to sleep like that, so we remove the wardrobe door from its hinges and push it under the mattress. By the time we have done this, most of the night has gone.

What little sleep we have is brought to an end at 6.00 am by two small boys pounding up and down the bare concrete corridor and staircase, whooping and hollering like Red Indians.

We have arranged for vegetarian meals, which means our breakfast is two hard boiled eggs each.

For the first couple of days, there is almost no snow at the resort. We are taken by coach to another where there is a sprinkling, and where we have to walk over a slippery metal bridge in our ski boots, to reach the piste. That's already a challenge even before we get to the snow.

On the third morning, we awake to a winter wonderland. Beneath a bright pastel blue sky, everything glistens white. The skiing is good, with plenty of gentle runs for Julie and myself, and sufficiently challenging ones for Terry. The weather is delicious, eating out is cheap, and one of Simon le Bon's brothers turns up with a group of friends, which keeps Julie happily occupied following them around.

We all ski every day and almost all day, lunching out at one of the many local restaurants. Meat-heavy menus offer us a limited choice of either a brik filled with egg or locally caught trout, both of which are delicious. The hotel continues to serve us hard boiled eggs for breakfast, and hard boiled eggs for dinner. Every day. I worry that we will become egg-bound.

Each evening when we return to our room, the bed has been neatly made. Nobody has remarked on the fact that the wardrobe door has been removed and replaced under the mattress.

We quickly learn to leave the slopes by mid-afternoon, because there is a limited supply of hot water in the hotel. Once it's used up, there is no more until next morning. One evening, as we are sitting down for dinner, a man wearing just a small towel around his loins comes running into the room, weeping.

He stands there holding the towel, sobbing.

Between sobs, he stutters: 'I can't take any more. I can't take any more. I want to go home. There's no hot water again!'

Somebody gets up and leads him out of the room. Once he's gone, a group of people start giggling between themselves.

The hotel is really pretty awful, but it doesn't matter because the skiing is so good. I am quite confident now skiing on the lower slopes, which are very wide and long.

Today, I decide to try a new run. It's a little more demanding but I feel like a challenge. Terry comes with me, and I start off OK until I lose my balance and fall over. While I'm sitting on the ground untangling my skis and poles, I glance behind me. Racing down the piste, clearly either out of control or blind, a large man is heading straight for me, despite the piste being half a mile wide. He is making no effort to change direction. Terry positions himself just behind me and plants his skis hard into the snow, so that the skier hits them rather than me. The man tumbles a long way and then picks himself up, shouting something foreign over his shoulder before he skis away.

I tell Terry to leave me and go and enjoy himself. That I can perfectly well manage. He skis off, I find my feet and set off once again. I realise now that the piste is actually quite a lot steeper than I had imagined and it's icy in places. For a short while, I hold it together until I have to swerve to avoid somebody who for some reason is just standing on the piste. That's when I wobble sideways and fall over again, where instead of stopping I keep on sliding. As I near the bottom of the slope, I see a pair of legs. I manage to hook my arm around them, bringing myself to a stop and annoying the owner of the legs who shouts at me.

I'm very frustrated that I couldn't manage what is classed as a green run and therefore something that should have been easy. All my previous confidence has vanished, so I decide the thing to do is try again.

It's a button lift, and at least I can easily ride those now. I grab hold as it comes past and let it tow me towards the top of the piste. There is a part of it where to the left there is a high snow bank, and to the right a line of straw bales that defines the edge of the lift track, which is only just sufficiently wide for one person. All goes well until a woman four buttons ahead of me falls off. There is nowhere for her to go, so she is lying crumpled between the snow bank and the straw bales. People are yelling at her to move and poking at her with their ski poles, but she obviously can't move. Consequently, the person behind her is dragged into her, the person behind them falls onto them, and the person behind them adds to the pile of people. By the time I arrive, the button is jerked sideways by the heap and I fall off face down into the frozen straw bales. The person behind me is dragged into me and knocks me over the edge of the bale, which scrapes my wrists painfully, and then I am sliding down a steep slope onto the piste.

My skis have remained attached, and I'm on my stomach sliding through the snow with my legs bent up behind me at an unlikely angle.

When I come to a stop, I bring my legs back to where they belong. I sit in the snow and laugh until the tears freeze on my face, imagining what it looked like to anybody watching. Meanwhile, back on the button lift, the bodies are still piling up. There's a lot of shouting and cursing.

I pick myself up and make my way back down in my inimitable fashion. I watch as a Bobcat drives up to where the fallen woman lies, two men collect her and put her onto a cradle and speed away with her. The other fallen people pick themselves up and find a button as the lift begins to work again.

Later, we learn that the poor woman had managed to break both legs when she fell.

After eight days of having boiled eggs for breakfast and dinner, we're hoping that for New Year's Eve the hotel will surprise us with something a little different, which they do.

The waiter presents our meal with a flourish and says he hopes we will enjoy it. We stare at the two vast bowls of creamy mashed potato, both studded equidistantly with six hard-boiled eggs.

There is cake for dessert. We take it out into the streets and stand with the crowds, drinking pink champagne as one year dies and a new one is born.

On the final day of our holiday, Terry disappears right up to the top of the mountain while Julie and I decide to relax on the lower slopes. We sit on the balcony of a restaurant, watching the beginners' class.

The ski school is part way up the mountain, on a plateau. To reach the plateau, the beginners have to take a button lift up quite a steep slope – in fact it's part of a black run.

A group of eight emerge from the hut for their first time on skis. The instructor leads them to the button lift. The buttons are quite high, requiring passengers to do a little jump to climb onto them. On this, their first time on skis, they are having to deal with them, as well as the ski poles attached to their wrists. They have to grab the pole of the button, slide the button between their legs and keep their skis parallel as the button moves up the hill.

Some of them snatch tentatively at the pole as it moves past, others grab on straight away. Not all of them manage to straddle the button, so they are dragged helplessly for a few yards before being forced to let go, then slide and slither backwards down to where they began. Their instructor has gone on ahead and is waiting at the top for them.

None of them get very far before they fall off part way up. They pick themselves up and turn around to go back to the bottom. As they have never skied before and don't know how to turn or stop, the moment they stand up, the skis take control and shoot down the hill, crashing into small shrubs and rocks that stick up through the snow. Sitting on the terrace in the sun with a mug of hot chocolate, Julie and I have bets on who will fall off next.

A woman almost reaches the top before she falls off the button and struggles to her feet. One of her skis has come off and slid out of reach. On her remaining ski, she tries to walk down to recover it, then falls on her back. She pulls off the ski and slides down on her bottom towards the one that has got away. Once she has retrieved it, she puts the two skis together and steps into them, so off they go again, rushing her down to the bottom of the hill into the queue waiting for the lift.

I can't remember a time when I have ever laughed quite so much at the misfortunes of others, because I can see myself doing exactly the same. It was the most fun I had on a skiing holiday and it was then that I decided that in future I'll regard it as a spectator sport.

23. That Sinking Feeling

A couple of days before Natalya produced her litter of pups, we took her with us to see the spectacular Severn bore. She was a roly-poly little barrel and Terry had to lift her over a style to reach the banks so we could watch the bore as it passed. It's caused by a high tide from the Atlantic Ocean forcing itself up through the increasingly narrow Severn estuary until it forms a spectacular wave, rolling over the river water passing in the opposite direction.

This part of Gloucestershire is a favourite place for our walks, and now that Natalya's pups are old enough to venture out, we often bring them all here. We've kept three of the eight for ourselves. Their first outing was along the tow path beside the canal. As soon as they saw the water, they rushed towards it, jumped in and were surprised to find they were unable to walk upon it. Terry had to haul them out as they paddled around in panic.

Today, we take them down to the mudflats and sandflats beside the river where they can safely run as far as they wish. It's a warm, sunny day. The dogs are racing around chasing each other and Terry is a little way ahead of me, to my left. I take a couple of steps towards the river, and the ground gives way beneath me. I am instantly up to my calves, and sinking. It takes a few seconds to realise that I've stepped into quicksand. I scream to Terry, at the same time shooing away the dogs who have come to investigate. The sand is slurping me down and has reached my knees.

Terry tosses me one of the long dog leads so I can grab one end, and he pulls me free.

Stepping into quicksand is horrifying because it happens so quickly. It's instant. There's no warning. One minute you're on terra firma, the next you are being swallowed by a silent force that has wrapped itself around you.

That's something I never want to do again.

24. Things That Go Clicketty-Clack in the Night

There are many excellent camp sites within less than an hour's drive from our home in France, which means we can get away for a short break, taking the dogs with us, and one of us going back to the house twice daily to feed and clean the parrot.

We go for a trial run with Dobby and Tally, to see how feasible it will be to take them camping and spend three days under canvas. Although they have to be kept tied whilst on the site, there are ample walks where they can be off the lead, and they behave very well when they are tethered. Usually very protective of us and their territory, they seem to soak up the calm, laid back atmosphere of the camp site and relax completely, lying at our feet while we read, sleeping beside us on the floor at night.

After this success, we take them away for a week to the small town of La Souterraine in the lovely Limousin.

The campsite is adjacent to a pine forest and the public park where there is a lake with a sandy beach and swimming area. With no road traffic, the dogs are able to run freely and cool off in the lake.

It is midnight. From the far distance comes the faint murmur of motorway traffic, and from closer, the yipping of a fox.

I need a wee and remember too that I did not brush my teeth earlier. Although the torch has new batteries, it glows weakly as if already exhausted, and we have not yet started the fifty-yard trek to the sanitary block. I zip myself out of the tent and follow the dim haze past the guy ropes, across the path, over the playground and down the rustic steps to the sanitary building. The night is eerily quiet and dark.

As I close the lavatory door, a loud, rapid clacking noise approaches, making me jump. It sounds like angry castanets. It stops outside my cubicle, and then slams the adjacent door, which emits an agonised screech like all the souls in hell falling into the eternal flames.

I quickly flush and run to a basin to brush my teeth before whatever it is emerges, but within seconds the squealing door is flung open, making me jump again. Out totters a wraith, staggering towards me, clutching its tummy. All in white, except for high-heeled gold sandals, the slender, blonde phantom has a shiny pale complexion, like a church candle. She reaches out a clawed hand and grabs at my basin.

'It's a *gastro*. From my daughter. Every time we go away, she has a *gastro*, and every time she gives it to me. Being in a tent and having a *gastro* – it's the worst possible thing.'

She bends double. '*Oh, mon dieu*, what pains in the stomach and the rest,' she fans the air behind her, and wrinkles her nose.

I am so transfixed by my new friend and her *gastro*, that I have forgotten I must brush my teeth gently, and always away from the gums. Instead, I've given them a thorough scrubbing. Our new effervescent toothpaste is fizzing and expanding in my mouth like that foam used for filling gaps around window frames. There is no room for it in my mouth any longer, and I have to spit, which I do as elegantly and noiselessly as possible, out of consideration for the wraith. We both gaze into the basin at the result – a cloud of blood-stained foam. She shrinks away from me with a gasp. I'm glad – as she has pointed out, there is nothing worse than having a *gastro* when living in a tent, and I don't know whether the *gastro* germs can travel through the air.

The wraith clicketty-clacks quickly away, still clutching at her middle, while I wash my hands for several minutes, and then my face and arms, just to be sure.

I tap my way back to the tent, shaking the torch violently to force a meagre gleam from it. In its dying moments – the batteries have lasted for all of four minutes – I notice something thick and dark clinging to the mosquito netting inside the bedroom. With a really hard whack, I wring a final spark from the torch, sufficient to find my way to the electric light switch.

Twenty centimetres from Terry's face, a savage-looking, robust spider, three centimetres long, two wide, is playing some sort of game with its legs, lifting them up one after the other.

With the assistance of a small bowl and a chopping board, Terry traps the spider and relocates it twenty yards into the hedge.

We are zipped up again. It is very dark, and somewhere I am sure I can hear a spider muttering to itself as it tries to open the zip.

25. Like a Holiday in a Car Wash

While we have always enjoyed camping, my chronic back pain has made bending down uncomfortable and occasionally impossible, likewise getting up from a low bed. We decide to buy a caravan which will allow us to travel as far and often as we wish, taking the parrot and keeping us and the dogs comfortable.

For its first outing, we take it to a caravan site fifteen miles from home. We drive there on a hot sunny day, set up the awning, take the dogs for a walk, sit in the evening sun having supper and a drink, and retire to bed.

We wake in the night to water dripping on us from the open skylight. It is pouring with rain. Really heavy rain.

In the morning, the awning is collapsing beneath the weight of water. We let it down and it forms a small lake around our feet. The rain hammers down all day until late evening, when we take the dogs for a walk and manage to get back to the van before the next wave of rain moves in.

By mid-morning on the third day, we have read all our books and are tired of playing cards while the rain lashes and the wind rocks, so we give in and pack up, dragging the soaking awning inside the caravan and heading home from what has seemed like a holiday in a car wash.

A few weeks later, we travel down to the Landes on the Atlantic coast.

The large parrot cage won't fit through the door of the caravan, so we buy a collapsible dog crate. This provides a very large space for Rafiki, who takes to it immediately. She travels in a cat box until we reach the campsite, where she goes very happily into her temporary home beneath an oak tree next to the caravan.

The Landes is a gorgeous, gorgeous part of the world, with hundreds of miles of pine forests and wide sandy beaches. Although it's late in the season and the beaches are almost deserted, the weather is fine and mild. Tally and Dobby run until they can't run any more. We are tucked away in a grove of oak, pine and bamboo, our only neighbour being a tall gentleman called Sarah who wears pink frocks and long dangly earrings. Sarah is elusive and seldom seen, except when they come out to submerge themselves in their own inflatable swimming pool.

That remains in my memory as the most relaxing holiday we spent with the dogs and Rafiki. Most unusually, nothing went wrong.

26. Spain – The Scenic Route

Last year, our friend Miguel lent us his apartment between Barcelona and Valencia on Spain's Orange Blossom coast. We had such a great stay in the little town of Alcossebre, that now we have a caravan we are going back there with the dogs.

Sadly Dobby is no longer with us, but we have a new family member, Tommy, a rescued Hungarian Vizsla. He was in a shocking state when he was rescued from where he had been left chained to a radiator, with no food, no water and no way of even sitting down. After six months of care by the French SPA, he was still thin and scabby when we brought him home. A soft bed, good food and loads of love has turned him into a copper-coated, spring-loaded bundle of joy.

The day before we leave on the 500-mile drive to Alcossebre, the south-east corner of France is hit by floods causing widespread devastation, so we have to change our usual route, instead heading south to San Sebastian and from there diagonally across Spain to our destination.

We're late leaving, and I have no idea why we have three different GPS systems plus a navigation app on a tablet all proposing different itineraries. We are going in ever-diminishing circles in sync with the ever-diminishing daylight. By the time darkness falls, we are still far from the Spanish border, trundling around in the Landes. I am becoming increasingly angry with the GPS systems and their disagreements with each other, and equally angry with Terry for insisting on using them all.

We find a site where we can stay the night and leave early next morning. I imagine we'll be installed in comfort on the Orange Blossom Coast by late afternoon.

I know now why each of the GPS devices is giving conflicting information. They are variously set for shortest, fastest, most economical and non-toll routes. Naturally, it is somewhat confusing, but refusing to be confused, Terry takes first the fastest, changes to the shortest, and then to the easiest route – always avoiding tolls.

Thus we begin an enchanting tour of the Pyrenees, which as you may know is one of my favourite regions of France. The landscape is just glorious, gentle mountains, gushing springs, tropical vegetation, mists hugging the mountain tops, lush, green, rich, majestic. Following the easiest route, we drive up and down and around and around the Pyrenees for several hours, uphill, downhill, around narrow bends and along little stony paths that grow smaller and stonier the further we go.

In our planning, one thing we had not planned for was carrying a Spanish map. With four different GPS systems, it seemed unnecessary. One of the GPS systems keeps losing the signal. The other can't find the roads we are on – I think its maps must be out of date. The third one has a rather abrupt tone which we don't much care for, and none of them can display a map of Spain larger than 3" x 2", thus we have no idea where we are. I have a vague recollection from a previous trip that we should go to Pamplona and from there to Zaragoza, or the other way round, then on to Barcelona and onto our destination.

So we head towards Pamplona, and then we head to Zaragoza, and the hours pass. It seems we are forever driving through bleak and barren mountains. Each time I check the remaining distance, the working GPS says 300 miles and eight hours. We keep seeing the same signs pointing to places we have already driven through. Once again we are in mountains. Where are the famous plains in Spain?

When we hit yet another mountain range, I crush a small spark of anger and frustration as the road winds up and up and back on itself, and up and up some more.

'What's the altitude?' asks Terry.

'820 metres,' I reply, thinking angrily that if it wasn't for the damned floods we'd have come by the original route, and not only would we be at sea level the whole way, but we'd have arrived and had a leisurely meal by now, instead of climbing these awful roads.

Night begins to fall. We climb ever higher. Surely there must be an end to mountains; they cannot just keep on going forever. As soon as we crest one, another one pops up ahead.

It's dark now, and we're up at 1200 metres with only ninety kilometres left to go.

Then GPS tells us to turn left, which we do, and astonishingly, we are in mountains AGAIN! I am so angry that I'm shaking.

By 10.15 pm, we have reached the town. We follow the signs to the campsite which leads to a rough road that deteriorates into a rocky pathway strewn with boulders, holes and gulches formed by storms. If I hadn't read a warning in the guide before we left, I wouldn't have believed this track was navigable. On and on it goes, every yard causing the suspension to groan and the crockery and cutlery in the caravan to shake and rattle. Something falls out of a cupboard and lands with a crash.

I am ready to burst into tears when we see the entrance to the campsite, and give a triumphant little laugh. We've finally made it!

There is a sturdy wrought iron gate 7ft. high, which is locked. There is nobody to be seen. I find a bell and a man appears on the balcony above us. 'One minute,' he says.

Down he comes, and although we have plainly got him out of bed, because he is wearing pyjamas, he is as civil and helpful as one could expect under the circumstances. He leads us through the sleeping site to our pitch.

It takes a long time to reverse the caravan in the dark, but eventually it is parked, the dogs are attended to, and when they are settled, we go for a calming walk beneath the stars.

In the meantime, the gate has been locked again and we are on the wrong side of it.

Once again I ring the bell, and once again the pyjamaed man comes down and lets us in, giving us a card that operates the gate. He asks, with an understandable touch of sarcasm, whether we will be needing anything again tonight.

We assure him he'll not hear a squeak from us ever again, and tiptoe back to the caravan, falling asleep instantly.

Early next morning, we take the dogs down to the sea, where the sun bounces off the waves in dazzling flashes. It's incredibly hot. Soon the dogs are panting, I'm dripping, and the skies over the mountains behind us have darkened in just a few minutes from blue to grey to purple and black. I can hear distant cracks of thunder.

'Let's get the awning up before the rain comes,' I say.

We try. We really, really try, but nothing seems to fit where it should, the poles keep collapsing, bits go missing, and the storm breaks.

The rain hammers down, lightning lights up the hills and the thunder roars furiously.

By the time the thing is finally up, we are both drenched and Tally is a quivering, shaking, trembling, panting wreck. I've always wondered why some dogs are so scared of a natural phenomenon.

When the storm blows itself out, we go to the office to complete the formalities. The computer is down. The internet is down. The electronic gate isn't working. The receptionist laughs and asks if we are enjoying the Spanish weather. There hasn't been such a ferocious storm as this for many years. It was unusual.

We drive down the track which is almost impassable now, and have a drink and meal at a restaurant we know from our previous visit. The owner comes over to chat. The storm is the talk of the town. In seventeen years, he'd never seen anything like it. Lightning had hit the TV satellite dish three buildings away and blown the dish across the street.

By mid-afternoon, the weather is restored to normal service, pleasantly warm with just a light breeze coming off the sea. This dog-friendly campsite is situated in the Sierra del Irta natural park which is home to a vast range of rare and unusual plants. There are many paths and small rocky coves, and one fairly level tiny beach where Tally likes to paddle. Tommy overcomes his initial astonishment at the sight of the sea and is beginning to enjoy getting his feet wet.

142

After its eventful beginning, this has turned out to be a perfect, relaxing holiday. The town itself has plenty of good restaurants, and although the dogs aren't allowed on the main beach, there are plenty of places where we can take them to run. In the evenings, there is the pleasure of walking down the promenade beside the sea and enjoying a nice Sangria. Alcossebre is such a friendly, peaceful town and we have had such a blissful stay there that instead of dragging the caravan home, we decide leave it in safe storage locally so we can come back again next year.

27. No Man's Land

It's a couple of years since we left the caravan in Spain, and our plans have changed. One reason is that Tommy has begun to hate travelling in the car, squealing and whining constantly, so it kills any idea of driving him more than 500 miles for a holiday.

We are going to drive to collect it, bringing it home so that we can site it somewhere nearby and start to use it again. We will drive down, pick it up, sleep for a few hours and bring it straight back home. Our neighbour will feed the dogs while we are away. It's a simple plan, and those of you who know us, or have read my books, will hear warning bells going off.

Our journey down is almost trouble-free, except for a slight quirk in our car which occasionally sets itself in a slow mode, for which nobody can find a solution. Switching off the engine and restarting gets it going again.

The address of the site where the caravan is stored is vague. We can't find it and go to the nearest town, which is like something from the Wild West. There is almost no sign of life, apart from a few people sitting outside buildings with their hats tipped over their faces. As we pass, they raise the brims to watch us suspiciously. It feels rather menacing. I go into a small store, buy a couple of cold drinks and show the address to the unsmiling man who serves me. He takes it, makes a phone call and holds up ten fingers. Shortly, a thin man drives up and signals us to follow him to a field surrounded by a collapsing wire fence, where we find the caravan looking somewhat the worse for wear. All the tyres are flat. The man lends us a pump, so once they are inflated, we hitch up and drive away.

With its twin axles, the van tows beautifully and we are batting along nicely. The car is running well, and we intend to keep driving through the night to get back home to the dogs. However, after driving for three hours, we are still south of Barcelona and starting to get tired. We decide to stop overnight and leave early next morning. We come to rest at Calafell – a large well-organised and well-maintained site with excellent amenities, just a thirty-second stroll to the fabulous beach.

As soon as dawn breaks, we have a quick cup of coffee, then hitch up and move away. The noise startles people within a radius of 100 yards, as the engine clatters and thumps, sounding like a tin can in a spin drier. Some smoke escapes from the bonnet.

Terry recognises that the alternator has failed, as the battery is not charging and warning lights and messages keep coming on. My suggestion of calling a garage is overruled because everything seems to be closed on Sunday. We must get back for the dogs and there happens to be another battery in the caravan that we can connect when this one runs out. We'll see how far we can get.

We bumble along. I make one navigational error that leads us into a fifty-mile stretch of narrow, winding roads, hairpin bends with coaches coming round them, warnings of falling rocks and jumping deer, and one mountain after another, but the car pulls gamely on until we are able to get back onto the motorway. When the battery finally dies, Terry changes it over and off we go again.

Five hours and 120 miles after leaving Calafell, we pass La Jonquera and are half a mile from the French border when the car starts missing very badly, coughing and spluttering. It grinds to a halt, on a bend up a hill, and rolls slowly backwards, crashing the caravan into the metal safety barrier.

The temperature is just below 100F, and my feet and hands have swollen almost beyond recognition. No knuckles are visible, and my feet are oozing out of my trainers.

Because the battery is dead, we can't open the boot to get out the compulsory red triangle. Instead, Terry puts the only red item we can find – a red thermos flask – on the road to warn traffic.

I pick up Terry's phone to call our worldwide assistance. Nothing happens. No ringing tone. Zilch. The battery is flat. I hate mobile phones, they never seem to work for me.

Cars hoot as they pass. Inside our car is a furnace. Outside is dangerous, with high speed traffic shooting past in both directions.

Things start to get better, before they will start getting worse again.

When you are obviously broken down in a dangerous situation, you imagine that sooner or later somebody will stop to help, or at least notify the nearest police. Perhaps, something will happen and help will arrive, but in this instance, apart from hooting angrily, nobody does anything.

Burrowing around in my handbag, I find a little white plastic mobile phone I carry for emergencies and have never used. Miraculously, it has a full battery, and actually connects to a lady at our breakdown insurance company.

She keeps asking for our GPS coordinates, which we don't have because the battery is flat and our GPS isn't working. I explain numerous times that we are on the N11 half a mile from the French border. Although she is as helpful as she can be, she cannot locate us on her system which only covers France, which we are not quite in. We are both getting frustrated, and I'm in danger of losing my temper or bursting into tears, because I am very, very big, now, from the heat, scarlet in the face and soaked in perspiration.

A scooter pulls up and a man walks towards us, asking whether we need help. He takes the phone from me and has a go at explaining our location. Eventually, the lady pinpoints us. She will call out a breakdown vehicle, but it may take some time.

While we are waiting, our new friend introduces himself: his name is Pascal, he lives in Perpignan and has been to La Jonquera to buy cigarettes, which cost half the price there than they do in France. He is concerned that we do not have the obligatory red triangle, and when I explain that we can't get it out of the boot, he says he will go back to La Jonquera and notify the police. When he returns, he says the Spanish police didn't seem interested in the fact that there was a car broken down on a bend on a hill, and neither were the French police at La Jonquera.

They didn't have a red triangle in their car.

It is impossibly hot, and he is wearing biking leathers. I thank him for stopping, and urge him to carry on now that we know the breakdown vehicle is coming, but he insists on waiting until it does, an hour later. With a handshake and a '*bon courage*,' he drives off. One of the great things about predicaments is that you generally meet the kindest and most helpful people, and it's a shame that they pass out of your life before you get to know them better.

Our breakdown insurance mentions that it will get us home from anywhere in Europe, so when the recovery vehicle arrives we can sit back and relax, once the car is loaded and the caravan attached. The driver announces he is taking us to a garage in Argeles-sur-Mer, because although our insurance promises to get us home from anywhere, it doesn't apply to our vehicles.

I can hear the driver telling the garage that our alternator is dead and that we want them to replace it. I stop him. We do not want the garage to replace the alternator. We want them to recharge both our batteries, and we will get the car home. The garage reply that without an alternator, the car won't move. I reply that it will have to. It's brought us 120 miles, and with a couple of recharged batteries it should continue to get us closer to home.

When we reach the garage, there is a belligerent little man waiting for us. He's aggressive and insolent and I'd like to whack him around the ears, but instead I ask politely if he will be kind enough to recharge our batteries, for which we will happily pay him. He replies that it will take all night, and we'll just have to wait. We ask him for a quotation for repairing the car – for insurance purposes – and he says he will do that in the morning. He's really quite intimidating, standing unreasonably close to me, trying to stare me down and clearly not going to be any more helpful than he absolutely has to be.

Luckily, the garage is in a clean, peaceful area, and the caravan has been put on a spacious car park just outside. There's a large car transporter parked there too, and a friendly English driver comes over to chat and hand us a couple of bottles of beer.

Before long, we are friends and walk the short distance into town for a pizza. I jam my feet into the trainers with difficulty. Because we were expecting to be back home by now, I'd only packed a toothbrush. No change of clothes. I am aware of looking frightful and being rather unfragrant.

We find a small restaurant and sit at a table on the pavement. Inside, they're watching a football match – England vs. Iceland. Our new friend, Phil, transports prestige cars all over Europe, from Lapland to Portugal. He shows us photos of some of the vehicles he has delivered – Bentleys, Aston Martins, Lamborghinis. When he delivered Lewis Hamilton's McLaren P1 to Monaco he left a note in the glove compartment saying that his young son was a fan and had hoped to get the driver's autograph. Within a couple of days, Hamilton had telephoned and chatted at length to the little boy, sending him his autograph together with a beautiful scale model of the car.

While we are eating, a handsome, fit man comes over and introduces himself, asking whether he may join us. He speaks fluent English with a slight American accent. He also speaks five other languages fluently, plus his native French, and says he's studying another two. He is a money market trader, and we talk for a couple of hours about Brexit, sport and life in general. He buys us all a round of drinks, and shares Terry's pizza; he's charismatic, amusing, interesting and friendly. What are the chances of meeting not just one, but two such great people to spend the evening with and forget our problems for a while?

Although we have the caravan to sleep in, there is no access to water or electricity and no means of washing, so I use the restaurant's loo and splash some water from the hand basin on my face and arms. As we leave the restaurant, a group of people wave and smile. Somebody calls out 'Second Brexit for England – knocked out by Iceland.'

My feet are still alarmingly swollen and I hobble back to the caravan, which is like a furnace smelling of sweaty clothes and feet.

At 7.30 am next day, Phil comes to the caravan with two mugs of tea and some biscuits before he sets off on his way.

We go to the garage and ask if the quotation is ready. The secretary calls the unpleasant little man, who says he's not going to the trouble of writing a quotation for people who have asked him to charge batteries. The cost to get the car running will be 800 Euros that we don't have, plus it's 40 Euros for charging the batteries... and if we don't move the car and the caravan today, he'll start charging parking fees.

Our insurance will not pay to get the vehicles home, but Terry is determined to do so. He tells the garage man that he is going to drive the car and tow the caravan all the way to our home. The man laughs and says it is impossible. Nobody can drive a dead car. People who know Terry will also know that telling him something is impossible is an irresistible challenge to him. He'll get the vehicles home however long it takes, even if he has to drag them all the way with a rope. At least the caravan is well-stocked with food, and it's somewhere to sleep.

We agree that I'll return by public transport, courtesy of the insurance, because one of us has to get back to the dogs. The neighbour who is feeding them isn't particularly dog-friendly but I have phoned to assure them I will be back very soon.

The taxi will collect me in an hour, says the insurance lady, to drive me to Perpignan station where my tickets will be waiting, as indeed they are.

It's a pleasant journey and a treat for a lover of train travel like myself. On the first leg, I'm 'upstairs' on a double-decker TGV that follows the Mediterranean coast north-eastwards from Perpignan to Montpellier and on to Nîmes, where there's a rapid changeover to catch the ride up to Paris and Tours. The platform is heaving with people and luggage and I have to employ my elbows energetically to reach my carriage and settle with my Kindle, with the luxury ahead of almost five hours of nothing to do but read and relax.

At Valence, a group of cheerful men come and sit opposite me, passing around a wooden box filled with luscious golden apricots, for which I am really grateful. All I've had to eat so far today is a warm apple from the caravan.

They leave at Lyon and are replaced by a couple of polite youths with a giant bag of Maltesers. I'm not a chocaholic, but they are my favourites.

They don't open the bag, but leave it lying tantalisingly within my reach, on the table between us. I can't stop looking at and am silently salivating, trying to use my mental powers to make them open it and, out of courtesy, offer me one/some. That isn't working, so I smile at them and look at the Maltesers and raise my eyebrows, like our dogs do when they see something they want. That doesn't work either, although they do smile back. I'm beginning to feel rather aggressive towards them. I can barely stop myself snatching the bag, so I go to the bar and order myself a bowl of risotto and a small vodka.

I arrive at Tours ten hours after leaving Perpignan and catch a little Thomas the Tank engine for the final step to Poitiers, where the insurance lady assured me there would be a taxi waiting to drive me home. The driver is a Humpty Dumpty of a man, who is rude and unhappy at facing a long drive into the depths of the countryside and not getting home until after midnight.

My quotient of tolerance and good humour is running low. I'm worried about Terry, worried about the dogs, hungry, tired, noticeably giving off an aroma of sweat and still wearing the same clothes I was wearing four days ago. I close my eyes and lean back, leaving him to mutter to himself.

After a few moments, he asks about the weather in Paris. I say I haven't come from Paris, but from Argeles-sur-Mer. I explain how the car is broken down, my husband has to find a way to bring it back but I have to get home to our dogs.

As if I've waved a magic wand, he changes. He's a passionate animal lover. He has a five-month-old chocolate Labrador called Leo, who is adorable and always up to mischief. We spend the rest of the journey talking about pets and their various whims. By the time I reach home, we're best friends.

When I walk into the house, the dogs stare in astonishment, then delight, although I think they recoil a little from my feet.

Meanwhile, Terry is edging towards home, using one battery until it's flat, and swapping to the other one, stopping wherever he can to get them recharged and parking up to rest when he can. He phones regular updates. He's been travelling for two days now.

Yesterday, I broke down and cried. Not because I'm worried, or my feet are still too swollen to get into my shoes, but because of the overwhelming kindness of so many people. Strangers have offered to take Terry to their home for a meal and somewhere to sleep. Somebody offered to lend him a car, another was willing to drive down to try to help fix the alternator. People we had never met offered to buy the alternator for us, and we could pay them back as and when. A friend drove 100 miles to take him a new battery so that he finally arrived home. That really choked me up.

When you end up in a predicament, it is then when you find out how very kind people are and it gives your belief in the goodness of human nature a good boost.

The day after Terry makes it home, one of our good friends finds the problem, a broken pulley that costs fourteen Euros.

*****

The adventure doesn't end quite there.

Although there is no more than a small dent on the rear right of the caravan, it has moved the body out of alignment with the chassis, and the vehicle is condemned. We no longer have a caravan. Somebody buys it to use as a spare room for guests.

A few days later, Terry goes to visit and thank the friend who mended the alternator.

Their house is at the bottom of a steep dip. As he is only going to be stopping for a couple of minutes, he leaves the car at the top of the dip with the engine running and the handbrake on.

He's persuaded to have a coffee, and the couple of minutes grow into a quarter of an hour.

Sitting with his friends in their garden, unaware that the handbrake cable has stretched in the heat, he and they are surprised to see the car gliding slowly and relentlessly down the drive; it misses, by just a few inches, the luxury camping car parked there, bumps up over a kerb, hitting a concrete pillar and metal gate belonging to a neighbour's garden.

The concrete pillar is broken, the metal gate is broken, and so, sadly is the car.

28. Wrong Number

After a particularly gruelling week, I need something to make me smile, and it arrives early morning with an incoming Skype call while I'm still in bed.

I click to accept the call and see a blurry video. I grope for my glasses and the image comes into focus to show a tanned man sprawled on a lounger, naked except for a hand towel covering his groin.

Still only half-awake, as I'm peering to see who the caller is, the little towel is slowly peeled away.

The camera pans upwards to the caller's face, and there is one of our ex-neighbours who works in the Middle East and is gay. I'm surprised but quite broad-minded, so wondering if it's meant as a joke, I say 'Hello!'

I hear a gasp, and the call disconnects.

That'll be a wrong number then. Still, it does start my day off with a giggle.

29. Stolen Goods

Those who have read my memoir *I Wish I Could Say I Was Sorry* may recall that as a five-year-old pupil at the local convent school, I was an adept thief, or so I thought. I stole paper from other children's workbooks, their break-time pennies, a bible and a rosary, little knowing that I had been observed. Instead of being punished, I was rather spoiled and felt so bad that I never had any desire to steal anything, ever again.

I have had opportunities, and been tempted. In a five star hotel, I once found on a washbasin six exquisite and very valuable rings that somebody had removed to wash their hands, and forgotten. My first thought was to hand them in to reception, but the prospect of holding them in my hand stopped me. I didn't trust myself to touch them.

When I was working as a cleaner for a wealthy family, I did help myself to a chocolate from a large and expensive box that was open in the living room. I thought that as the box was left invitingly open, they wouldn't begrudge me just one. That has been the limit of my dishonesty until the day of the Topshop sale.

Our office is at Oxford Circus, just across from Topshop. Anybody who knows me well knows that I am not a shopper. I particularly hate clothes shopping, absolutely loathe it, much preferring to browse the rails and buy from charity shops. However, there is a sale at Topshop and a friend nags me into going with her. I end up in a changing room with an armful of clothes. After trying them all, I choose several and go to pay for them. Once I get home, I put the bag in a wardrobe to sort out when I have time. A few days later, I remember I've bought some new clothes and unpack them. The receipt in the bag lists four items, but I have five. I haven't been charged for a linen dress in shades of cream and brown.

The price ticket is still attached. £18, reduced to £9. I must either take the dress back or pay for it. As it's rather smart, I decide to keep it and fully intend to go and pay for it next day.

Then I think of spending my lunch hour fighting through the crowds, and queuing up to explain how I came to have a dress I haven't paid for, and the confusion this will cause the girl on the till, who will have to summon a supervisor to do something because she is not able to deal with payment for goods that haven't been paid for, and the more I think about it, the less I feel inclined to go through all the rigmarole. Then I reason that if Topshop are careless enough to undercharge, it's possible they are equally likely to overcharge, and how much difference will £9 make to them anyway? I put the dress on a hanger in the wardrobe and forget about it.

Many months later, we are invited to an event given by a Russian lady who has been working for us. She is a lovable extrovert personality with exquisite taste, but her recent divorce from a wealthy husband has seen her fortunes take a downturn, so she is now forced to work for a living. Plainly, selling life assurance isn't her forte, and she has so far not made any sales, although not from want of trying. This hasn't quashed her spirit and she is determined to rebuild her life. She has many contacts among the great and the good and entertains in style. At one of her dinner parties, our fellow guests include a titled gentleman of whom she is currently the mistress, a notoriously racist baroness and Germaine Greer. Ms. Greer doesn't speak to anybody for the entire evening, so I can't give any opinion on her.

Lara has met an Englishman and fallen madly in love with him. She is radiant and wonderful in her happiness, and she is going to make a public declaration and celebration of her love. She has hired a nightclub in Carnaby Street for a lunchtime event to which all her friends are invited.

I decide that the stolen Topshop dress will be a good choice to wear. It does look extremely smart, with a hemline just on my knees in keeping with the current fashion.

There are about eighty people seated around a central stage, where

Lara plays the perfect hostess, entertaining us with music and poetry readings. Then there's lunch, a buffet of entirely raw vegetables, finely sliced, which is a little odd and provokes some heckling from some of the rowdier guests. After we've all eaten and listened to some more music and recitals, the lights on the stage are dimmed, and a spotlight falls on Lara. She describes her life over the last few years, how her marriage failed, how she found herself alone and almost penniless, having to work for her living and feeling that life is over. And then, one magical day she sets off in the hope of selling a policy to a potential client and falls in love with him. It is a meeting of minds, bodies and souls and she wants all her friends to witness her public declaration of love to Martin.

She holds out her hands and beckons Martin onto the stage. He is the epitome of an introverted Englishman. Clearly mortified, he tries to resist, holding up both hands in a 'halt' signal, but Lara is insistent, laughing away his protests and pulling him up beside her. She picks up a parcel tied with a ribbon and addresses her audience.

'I am Russian, and in Russia red is the colour of love. Martin, I hereby pledge you my heart and my eternal love.' She hands him the parcel.

Martin takes the parcel, thanks her and moves to return to his seat, but she holds him back.

'Open it!' she cries.

Martin reluctantly pulls off the ribbon, opening the parcel to reveal a magnificently embroidered scarlet silk kimono. He thanks her again and tries to fold it back up, but Lara says:

'But you must put it on! Put it on so all our friends can see you.'

With his face as scarlet as the kimono, Martin puts it on over his corduroy trousers and jumper, then stands squirming with embarrassment, the kimono all akimbo. We can feel the crowd united in their sympathy for him.

Somebody cheers and claps, and we all join in as Lara kisses Martin passionately.

The celebration has been going on for four hours. People begin to stand to leave, but Lara motions everybody back into their seats.

'I have not finished yet,' she says. 'With all the difficulties I have had to cope with over the last year, it is the support of my friends that has seen me through these terrible times, and I thank all of you here today.'

She calls out a few names and invites them to join her on the stage.

We all clap.

'There is one couple,' she continues, 'whom I have to thank from the very bottom of my heart for their help and kindness, and I ask all of you to please join me in recognising them. Terry and Susie, please join me down here.'

Terry jumps up immediately, always happy to be in the limelight. I sit clinging to my chair, numb with horror. I wave, hoping that will satisfy Lara, but no.

'Come, come, come down here both of you,' she cries, signalling with her hands like a ground handler bringing an aircraft into its parking place.

I have never been so embarrassed in my life and wish the floor would open up and swallow me, but the horror is only just beginning.

Terry grabs my hand and pulls me to my feet.

During the four hours we have been sitting, the skirt of the linen dress has folded itself into tight horizontal accordion pleats. As I stand up, it springs up to reveal my underwear. Instead of reaching to my knees, it is now just a pelmet around my pelvis. Oblivious, Terry drags me down the stairs towards the stage. With my free hand, I try to retain my modesty.

I'm hauled up onto the stage, into the spotlight, wrenching my hand from Terry's grip so that I can battle the skirt with two hands, but no matter how I tug and pull at it, it bounces back. I bend my knees to try to lower the hemline. As I pull it down at the front it, rises at the back.

Our hostess enfolds us in her arms and shouts: 'Let's have a big round of applause for Terry and Susie.'

As the crowd clap politely, I stare into the spotlight like the proverbial rabbit in the headlights.

Even if my clothing was correct, I would have hated being the focus of attention; with the hideous stolen dress leaving me exposed from just below the waist, my mortification is complete.

Back at home that evening, I rip the dress apart at the seams, cut it up with scissors and throw it in the bin.

30. Fishy Business

We buy our fresh fish in bulk from a local supplier.

(Tip: Never buy 10 lbs. of skate wings unless you are present and able to wrap them individually. When our delivery arrives, we are on our way out, so put the box in the freezer to deal with on our return. We promptly forget it is there until the following day, ending up with a 10 lb. skate wing lollipop.)

Our supplier argues that frozen fish is fresher than fresh fish, as it is caught at sea and fast frozen in its prime, whereas fresh fish has to be caught, landed, sold to wholesalers, transported to market to be purchased by retailers, so by the time you buy it, it's already twenty-four hours old.

They are filming a presentation of their products, showing various methods of preparing fish. We are invited, so off we go.

I've been riding all morning. It's a rush to get to this afternoon's show, and I'm still in breeches and boots, but as we expect to be sitting in a dark auditorium, it won't matter.

The presentation is set up under the lights, in the form of a small kitchen and a little table and two chairs. The chef prepares varieties of fish in different ways. Now they need some people to come and eat it.

'Does anybody have a birthday today?' asks the presenter.

No reply.

'How about yesterday?'

No reply,

'Who has a birthday this week?'

No reply.

Then a voice calls out: 'We both have birthdays this month.'

'Wonderful', replies the presenter. 'Come on down here the two of you.'

Once again, Terry is dragging me into the spotlight, this time with the added bonus of film cameras. Although I'm wearing clothes that I have paid for, mud-spattered breeches and boots are not really appropriate wear for dining out. Still, at least we are seated and I'm only visible from the waist up, and wearing a clean T-shirt.

31. In the Spotlight

We are staying at the Gatwick Hilton prior to flying to Florida for a company convention. The huge lobby of the hotel is dominated by a suspended replica of the plane belonging to record-breaking aviatrix Amy Johnson. Your eye is immediately drawn to it. You cannot avoid looking up at it.

Our room is on the first floor, and opens out onto a wide, brightly-lit corridor which gives a close-up view of the suspended aircraft. For some reason, we have been given twin beds separated by a fitted table with tea and coffee-making equipment. After checking in in the afternoon, we have a cup of tea before preparing for the evening's dinner.

As always on these occasions, we are wined and dined splendidly, and Terry has particularly enjoyed the wine.

By bedtime, he falls instantly asleep and begins snoring contentedly and extremely loudly.

This is bad on two counts. Firstly I am misophonic and the sound of snoring sends me demented. Secondly, when I am kept awake, I am evil personified. The absolute total bitch from hell.

For a short while, I try to sleep by putting the pillow over my head and jamming my fingers in my ears, which is uncomfortable, painful in fact because my fingernails are sharp. I try shouting but it has no effect. Terry sleeps and snores on.

I get out of bed and go to try to turn him over, but he's too heavy, so I prod him hard with my sharp fingernails and tell him to shut up. By the time I've got back to my bed, he's off again.

I get angrier and angrier. I take the duvet and pillow and try to make a bed in the bath, but I can still hear the snoring and my anger level reaches murderous.

I pick up the teapot, which contains left-over tea, and can barely restrain myself from smashing it on his head. Instead, I pour the cold tea all over his face.

That wakes him up.

I get back into bed, turn off the light and hear him bumping around trying to find his way to the bathroom. I hear the door click closed behind him. With the snoring stopped, I have almost fallen asleep when he starts gently tapping on the bathroom door, presumably unable to find how to open it in the dark. I am desperate to get to sleep and pull the pillow back over my head, leaving him to tap. Although I can hear the tapping, it does not affect me in the same way as snoring does, so I do drift off to sleep. Alas, only briefly, because the tapping becomes louder and more urgent. Shaking with rage and cursing, I snap on the bedside lamp, leap out of bed and wrench open the bathroom door.

He isn't in there. I look across at the other bed, he isn't there either. He's nowhere to be found. He isn't in our room.

I hear the tapping again. It is coming from outside.

Opening the door onto the brightly-lit lobby with the suspended replica aeroplane, I find Terry flattened against the wall, stark naked and looking confused.

How long he has been out there neither he nor I know, but he mentions that several people have walked past him, looking at him oddly while he has been tapping on the door. Uncertain that it was the right door, he has tried several others too, none of which had opened, which is probably just as well or he may not have been able to join the flight next day.

Next morning when he wakes up, he says: 'Oh dear, I seem to have spilled tea all over the pillow.'

He has no recollection of his naked nocturnal adventure.

I don't say a word.

32. The Eerie Dark

I am driving from Nairobi to Mombasa with my then fiancé in a Fiat 500, a tiny little car known as the Topolino, 'the little mouse'. It's a 300-mile journey and we stop at the halfway point, Mtito Andei, where the pretty Tsavo Inn offers a good meal and a cool swim in the pool. We leave there at 11.00 pm, planning to drive the rest of the way slowly to reach Mombasa very early the following morning. There is little traffic on the road at this time of night.

We haven't been driving for long when the headlights pick out a dark shape on the road ahead.

At first it looks like a stationary truck, but it turns out to be a bull elephant waving its ears and swinging its head from side to side, sending a polite-but-firm message that we shouldn't try to go around it. We don't, and turn off the engine.

The Topolino weighs roughly one ton. An adult African elephant weighs between five and six tons. Eight more elephants appear on their silent spongy feet, brushing against the car and moving around it.

With the headlights switched off to save the battery, it is indescribably eerie sitting in the dark in a small tin box. It's frightening too, yet at the same time, magical and exciting. I can hear my heart beat, and the rumbling noises as the elephants communicate with each other. Every time the engine is started, the big bull on sentry duty sways a warning.

Two more vehicles arrive and line up behind us with their engines switched off. There we wait silently, in the dark, until a large tanker appears and slowly encourages the animals off the road so we can continue our journey.

It is a most magical moment that lasts no more than ten minutes, but remains one of my most beautiful memories.

33. Park Lane

It's the company's Christmas beano, and we are staying in the swanky Dorchester Hotel in London. Our room is enormous and sumptuous, with thick, heavy floor-length curtains to cut out the traffic noise and lights from Park Lane.

When I had first came to live in England, I had begun sleepwalking and having frequent nightmares that I was imprisoned. One night, I dreamed I was locked in a greenhouse and was telling myself not to worry because I could easily break the glass to get out. Then I heard somebody say: 'She thinks she can escape – but she doesn't know it's plexiglass and it's unbreakable.'

In my sleep, I had climbed out of bed and put my elbow through the bedroom window, ending up with shards of glass in my hair and dozens of small wounds on my arm.

The nightmares are now far less frequent although I do still tend to wander around in the night. As long as there is sufficient light for me to see where I am, I just get back into bed.

After our celebration dinner and dancing we go back to the splendid room and quickly fall asleep.

Some time later, I wake up and the room is in total darkness. There is not the smallest chink of light. I reach out to the bedside for a lamp, then pat the headboard to see if there's one there, which there isn't. Terry normally wakes if he hears me moving about, but he's in a deep sleep. I step out of bed onto the thick pile carpet and feel on the wall to try to find a light. I follow the wall, tapping on it, feeling for a light switch. I can feel my heartbeat accelerating. I turn around in the dark, become completely disorientated and begin panting. With my arms held out stiffly in front of me, I seek a wall, a door, a switch. I bang into something – a table or chair and feel around there. Surely there must be a lamp somewhere? I keep blundering around running my hands up and down and backwards and forwards on the walls, really panicking now because I feel I'm trapped in a box, and it's getting hard to breathe.

I'm certain I've examined every wall in the room, there is no way out and there is no light to turn on. I can't remember the layout of the room, having not taken a great deal of notice of it earlier. I can't find the bed now, and there's a moany noise in my throat, like a dog whining.

I stop being cautious and begin hurling myself around, striking out around me with my arms, until I feel the wooden panels of a door. Where there is a door, there is always a light switch nearby and I feel for it but can't find it. I find the doorknob and turn it, expecting it to open out into the corridor. I push the door and nothing happens. I pull it and nothing happens. I can't find a key, or a lock and the door will not open. We are locked in.

Then I totally lose it and start pounding with my fists on the door, screaming: 'Open this door and let me OUT!' at the top of my lungs.

From the other side of the door, a voice calls out: 'Be quiet, you stupid woman, and go to sleep.'

At the same time, Terry finally wakes up, asking where I am and what I'm doing.

I start crying, and reply that I don't know where I am because I can't find a light. I hear him moving about, then he finds a switch on the wall above the bed.

As the light comes on, I find I am standing in one corner of the room on the wall where the bed is. The door I am trying to break down is not the door into the corridor, but the door into the adjoining room, which can be opened up into a suite.

I open the curtains slightly, just sufficiently to let in a crack of light from the road, and go straight back to sleep.

When we are checking out next morning, the people in the adjoining room are just coming out into the corridor. We nod politely to each other. As they walk away, the man bends his head and speaks to his partner, who turns and takes a look at me. I expect they think I was drunk.

34. Drowning Not Waving

We are on a company convention in the Algarve in Portugal. The hotel is so newly built that it is not yet completed. Our room is on the third of four floors. The fourth floor is still under construction, still just a bare concrete roof. At the end of the corridor on our floor is a door, which opens out, with no warning, to a void leading down to the ground three floors below.

Horse riding is available, and Terry and I book a ride out for the two of us with a guide. At the stables, a group of wives and partners from our party are also mounting up ready for a lesson, laughing, most of whom never having sat on a horse before. They are wearing sun tops, shorts and sandals. One of them shouts gaily: 'Wheee, off we go!' and kicks her heels into her horse. It shoots off, disembarking her straight out of the side door. One of the other horses follows, also despatching its rider. One woman has a broken shoulder, the other concussion.

The horses, we learn, belong to the Portuguese show jumping team. They are highly bred, highly trained and high spirited, and totally unsuited to novice riders. It's unlikely they have ever been kicked in the ribs before today. How they came to be on hire for hotel guests I have no idea.

Terry and I go out for a ride with a guide. What an extraordinary privilege to be riding such magnificent horses. On loose reins they are relaxed and obedient, their heads held proudly, light on their feet, almost bouncing as if they are walking on clouds. The guide takes us along a jagged clifftop path where I notice the edge of the cliff is very crumbly; there are great lumps of it far below on the beach. Deep cracks run through protruding parts which look in imminent likelihood of falling away. My mount seems to be magnetically drawn to these edges as if it has suicidal tendencies. I have to keep steering it away.

Due to my almost total ignorance of Portuguese and his complete lack of English, when our friendly guide invites us to a visit next day, I think it is to a local dairy. It seems impolite to refuse because he seems so enthusiastic about it. Something clicks and I realise that he is in fact talking about a bull fight. So that's an emphatic '*Não obrigada*'.

Next day, we are taken on a boat to a deserted beach for a barbecue. The water is shallow so the boat has to anchor a little way off-shore, and we are ferried to the beach in small motor boats.

It's a pleasant afternoon, barbecuing freshly-caught sardines, washed down with plenty of wine. We dance on the beach and are all very mellow when it's time to leave. As it's a sunny afternoon and the sea is warm and inviting, quite a few of our group swim back to where the boat is anchored. When they have all gone, I make a late decision to follow them.

Terry takes my towel and sun hat in one of the motor boats, and tells me to shout out if I have any problem.

I'd go so far as to say I am probably worse at swimming than I am at skiing. Two widths of a swimming pool is my limit, but the boat is so close, I know I can easily reach it. I walk out into the shallow water until it reaches my shoulders, and then I begin swimming with my best breaststroke. I've never mastered the crawl because I hate having water in my face. I do about twenty strokes, by which time I can no longer touch the bottom, and the water is lapping gently into my face and up my nose, making me snort and splutter. I keep swimming, spitting out the water, and look up to the boat. I had expected it to be very close by now, but it looks as far away as it did when I started. In fact, if anything it looks even further away. I tread water for a minute, then start swimming again, already feeling tired and with my neck aching from keeping my face up out of the water.

I look to the motor boat where Terry is and try to attract his attention, but he doesn't notice. I look back at the beach and wonder if I should swim back there, but it looks quite far away, and there's nobody left. The boat seems still further away, as if it's moving slowly out of reach. I can feel panic starting to take over. I rest again, trying to keep my face above the water but it's really getting up my nose, and burning the back of my throat. There is no energy left in my body.

I know now that I could die unless I remain calm, so I keep treading water, waving my arms and legs gently like a sea anemone until I have regained a little strength, then I start swimming once more. I'm close enough now to be able to see the people standing on the deck, looking towards me. With a flood of relief, I raise my hand to wave, signalling that I need help. They all wave back, cheering.

The terrifying thought strikes me that the boat may leave without me, not noticing I'm missing, leaving me here too far from the shore to swim back, leaving me here to drown. I can feel tears surging and streaming out of my eyes. I am so, so frightened.

I think about just letting go, letting myself sink slowly to the bottom in this warm water. I wonder how long it would take, and if it would be as peaceful as people say, a gentle way to die. I don't have the energy to continue, but on the other hand, I can't bear the salt water getting up my nose and down my throat.

'Stay calm, or die,' I tell myself. 'If you panic, if you give up, you will sink out of sight before anybody even realises you're missing, and by the time they do it will be too late. This is real. Stay calm.'

I move my hands up and down to keep afloat while I rest and gain some more energy. I swim a few more yards, rest, swim a little more and am almost in touching distance of the boat. I can clearly hear people's voices chatting and laughing. The boat is bobbing gently in the water, and as I lunge at the metal ladder fixed to the side, the rungs whack into my shins. It's painful and wonderful. I hang on to the ladder for a couple of minutes, laughing and crying at the same time, then climb up onto the deck. I watch blood trickling from my shins, down my legs and between my toes, leaving red footprints on the deck. Nobody notices.

As near-death experiences go, it was as near as I would ever want to get again. Unless you are a strong swimmer certain of your ability, don't ever take a risk in water where you cannot touch the bottom, or have something to hold onto or somebody with you. The distances on water can be so deceptive.

35. Paris

Although we live thousands of miles apart, Jennifer and I have been really good friends since 1998, when I advertised on the Internet for someone to come and stay in our house and look after our animals while I was hiking across France (*Best Foot Forward*).

There were many replies. When Jennifer wrote that she would like to come, I answered that I felt it unwise for her to come so far, from Texas, to a country where she didn't know anybody and couldn't speak the language.

She replied: *Ticket booked, arriving 2nd May.*

We clicked the moment we met and have remained friends ever since. Jennifer comes to visit every few years, this is her second home, she has friends here and she loves being here. She's happy to simply relax in the house and garden, play with the animals and generally chill out. She is my most easy-going friend, always cheerful and skilled at calming me down when I explode or panic. We can sit and chat for hours or equally sit in silence. She's comfortable to be with.

This trip is to celebrate twenty years of our friendship. Before coming home to relax, we are going to spend three days exploring Paris. I'm thrilled to find a special deal on the TGV, where we can buy return tickets to and from Poitiers to Paris and back for a pittance.

Unfortunately, the SNCF go on strike and our trains are cancelled. It's disappointing; the train is my favourite means of travel. However, serendipitously a friend who lives nearby and works abroad is flying from Paris. He will have to drive up there to catch his flight the day before Jennifer's arrival, leaving him with the problem of how to get his car back home. That's where I come in, travelling up with him and keeping his car to drive back after we have done Paris.

I spend the night in an F1 hotel near the airport at Charles de Gaulle.

My room is small and furnished with the basic requirements, but it is inexpensive, sparkling clean with on-site parking and restaurants very nearby. The hotel operates a regular shuttle back and forwards to the airport which will save me driving there. If you are looking for luxury you won't find it here, but for convenience and value, I highly recommend it.

I'm crazily excited to see my friend tomorrow, so I have two large whiskies to ensure I sleep well. Next morning, I catch an early shuttle to the airport and have breakfast there while waiting for Jennifer's flight. She never seems to age. Every time I see her, she seems as young as she was the first time we met twenty years ago. No lines, clear skin, shiny eyes. Even after travelling for many long hours, she's as bright as a button. I wish I knew how she does it. Maybe it's the climate in Arizona where she now lives.

We take the shuttle back to the hotel and collect the car. I'm slightly apprehensive about the drive into town, but it's surprisingly easy and we reach our destination in the northern suburb of Paris in twenty minutes without difficulty.

We're staying at an Airbnb in a quaint little pine-panelled cottage in the garden of a large house near St Denis. It isn't the most affluent area of Paris, but it's peaceful, has off-road parking and public transport almost from the doorstep into the city centre. The population is diverse and cosmopolitan, and everybody we meet there is friendly. There's a small general store, a bakery selling beautiful breads and patisserie fifty yards away and a pizza restaurant two doors down.

The off-road parking involves driving down the narrowest space between two tall brick walls that I have ever seen, and then manoeuvring the vehicle into a minute space with concrete steps to one side and a large truck on the other. I can't see how the truck gets in and out. There is literally no room for error if I'm to avoid scraping the car. Left to myself and taking my time I can do it, but the owners of the property are determined to help. They both give directions, waving their arms, shouting, urging me forwards, then backwards and yelling warnings. I am reduced to a nervous wreck. The husband offers to park the vehicle for me, but then discovers it is an English car with the steering on the right-hand side, which he cannot get to grips with, and he also doesn't know how to drive a car with automatic transmission. He comes dangerously close to ploughing through a low garden wall, so I have to insist on him getting out. Thankfully this is where Jennifer takes over, and in a few seconds she has the vehicle neatly parked. I'm not even going to think about how we'll get out of here when we leave, because there is no room to turn and you have to reverse the whole way, but I'll leave that to Jennifer.

I don't know if she has ever panicked or lost her cool, but I suspect not. She is the coolest, calmest person I have ever known, with a soft, Southern accent. If something needs to be done, she'll make sure it is.

Having squeezed the car into place, we inspect our accommodation. It's smaller than it seemed in the photos, like a large doll's house. Particularly the shower which takes a considerable amount of effort and contortion to get into, but it has everything we need for our stay. I sleep up on a mezzanine, being extra careful not to turn over in the night because the bed is right on the edge of the steep staircase. Jennifer has the bed-settee downstairs.

We spend the first evening sitting and chatting, catching up since we last saw each other, rounding off the evening with a pizza and a couple of glasses of Pineau de Charentes, then turn in for an early night.

Jennifer has only expressed one wish while we are in Paris, and that is to see the Eiffel Tower. Apart from that we have no plans of what to see or where to go. We are going to go with the flow and take our time to enjoy the city.

My sweet friend Angela had posted me some travel vouchers which enable us to use all the public transport all day long. We can catch a bus two minutes from our accommodation, and enjoy travelling through the suburbs of Paris before we reach the centre.

Neither of us are shoppers, but we can't possibly not visit the temple of hedonism that is Galeries Lafayette, floor upon floor of luxury goods and fragrant fragrances. It is architecturally stunning, enchanting, and entertains us for fifteen minutes before we are back outside and getting lost.

After much roaming around and asking directions from local people (who are without exception friendly and helpful - where are the rude Parisians?), we make it to the Champs Elysées garden and sit in the sun eating crêpes, beside a couple dozing beneath a large black umbrella. Afterwards, we stroll up to the Arc de Triomphe.

With no agenda to stick to, it's a most relaxing day, just wandering around the streets and taking buses to get around. Due to terror threats, the Eiffel Tower has been fenced off. We can't get close, so find a man selling ice creams and decide to just sit in the Champs de Mars, watching the world go by. There's a group on an organised tour, being marched swiftly along behind a man carrying a bright orange flag on a stick; a fraught young man wrestling with a small vocal boy who has thrown himself to the ground screaming, and a crowd gathered around some men who are playing the three cup trick.

It clouds over slightly and we make our way down to the river for a cruise on the Seine. With all the extra security around the tower, there are hoardings, scaffolding and barricades, so we have to climb over a ditch where the road has been dug up. It's like a mini obstacle course.

The cruise gives us perfect views of some of the great sites of Paris – the Louvre, Notre Dame Cathedral, Musée d'Orsay, Conciergerie and Grand Palais. We enjoy it so much that we stay on it for a second trip.

Taking the bus back to the apartment later in the evening, we are amused to see an elegant woman and a young girl, laden with gold jewellery and half a dozen designer shopping bags. They settle into seats opposite us, then the woman opens a large brown paper bag, takes out and eats a giant McDonald's burger.

I thoroughly enjoy travelling through the suburbs and seeing the 'other' side of Paris, with its colourful, multicultural shops and inhabitants.

Next day, we're back on the bus for more mooching around, stopping for coffees and cakes, and lunch in a small bistro. Feeling very French!

As our close up view of the Eiffel Tower yesterday was thwarted by all the boarding around it, we take a bus to Trocadero for a perfect, unimpeded view of the tower and the beautiful symmetry of the Champs de Mars. I'll admit that the first time I saw the tower in real life, I thought it was ugly, but I've mellowed. Although I still can't describe it as beautiful, it is so much a part of the Parisian skyline that I'd miss it if it wasn't there.

There are two things that Jennifer particularly enjoys: one is Pineau de Charentes, and the other is ice-cream, so we decide to grace a pavement table at popular Café Kléber. The waiter glances our way and ignores us, but that's OK because we are happy to sit in the sun watching Parisians going about their business. Inside the restaurant is empty, and there are a couple of vacant tables next to us, so maybe we are being ignored because we are obviously tourists. Nobody is more skilled at snubbing unwanted guests than a French waiter.

Eventually he gives in and comes to ask what we want. Ice-cream, we tell him. Ah no, he's sorry, they are only serving lunch (it's 2.30 pm) and it isn't possible to just serve ice-cream. I smile back and say that's OK, we'll just sit here patiently and wait until lunchtime is finished. We do this for ten minutes, then he relents with a small shrug, and returns with a menu. We order a couple of drinks and two of the most expensive small ice creams in the Western world. Still, they are very good.

Without any pressure to be anywhere particular at any particular time, this was a perfect way for two good friends to spend two days exploring and enjoying the City of Light at leisure. If you stroll around anywhere, you can't avoid the sights, sounds and smells that make Paris the glorious city that it is.

36. Berlin

If anybody had suggested a few years ago that I'd choose a holiday in a major European city, I'd have scoffed. I don't enjoy shopping at all and avoid it wherever I can. Neither do I find pleasure in traipsing around landmarks, so why have we ended up in Berlin, in October?

It's late in the year for a seaside holiday, easyJet are selling return tickets from Bordeaux to Berlin for 50 Euros, Terry is particularly interested in WWII history, and I like a holiday where I can learn something.

We've booked an Airbnb in the affluent, leafy suburb of Zehlendorf, south-west of Berlin city. I've lost the directions our host gave for getting there from the airport, so we climb on to the nearest bus, which is full of teenage schoolchildren.

My knowledge of German is limited to *danke, bitte, schöne, guten morgen, guten nacht, reifen* and *düngemittel fabrik*. I show the address to a couple of schoolgirls, who look at it and say something I don't understand. Then a boy steps forward and in perfect English explains that we are heading in entirely the wrong direction. He carefully writes down instructions that will put us back on track if we leave the bus at the next stop, which we do.

Our accommodation is in a large modern house that is sparkly clean, light and airy. Everybody takes their shoes off whenever they enter. There is an automatic lawnmower trundling quietly around the garden, and squirrels leaping in the branches of the trees. Adina, our friendly and helpful hostess drives us to the nearest supermarket so we can stock up our breakfast supplies for the next week. She also gives us a useful map of the Berlin public transport system, which, once we have worked it out (it's all in German) makes simple work of planning our activities each day.

For 34 Euros each, we buy a ticket that gives us unlimited travel on all the public transport systems - trains, buses, trams and underground. A three-minute walk from the house takes us to the bus stop, five minutes later we are at the quaint Art Nouveau train station of Mexikoplatz. From there, it's a twenty-minute ride into Alexanderplatz, the main public transport hub in Berlin from where you can get anywhere either by bus, train or underground.

If the train is scheduled to arrive at 11.26, that is precisely the time it arrives. If the bus timetable says the next bus will be in eighteen minutes, that is when it arrives. It is a testament to my confidence in Berlin's transport system that I voluntarily ride on the U-bahn underground train.

Our first day of sightseeing starts with Berlin's Botanical Gardens. The gardens cover more than 100 acres and include a collection of magnificent 19th century glasshouses. The weather is sunny and warm, the autumn colours are at their most vibrant, and the only other signs of life we meet as we explore the different areas of the garden are some playful squirrels and rabbits, numerous birds and a couple of foxes. We could have spent most of the day here, it's so beautiful and peaceful, but after we've had a coffee at the restaurant, Terry's interest begins to wane, so we take a train ride to the Brandenburg Gate.

There a man stands balanced on the saddle of his bicycle, with one arm raised in a victory salute beside a poster strapped to a post. It seems to be some kind of political statement, but it's in German so we are none the wiser. He is a young man with a splendid, tanned physique, of which we can see virtually everything, as all he is wearing is sunglasses, trainers, socks and a minuscule blue cotton elephant trunk to preserve his modesty, which doesn't leave a great deal to the imagination. We'll see him there again tomorrow.

From the Brandenburg Gate, we walk through the Tiergarten, where a man is standing blowing bubbles, to the German Resistance Memorial Centre. Even with Google maps, it isn't very easy to find as it's tucked away in a block of office buildings, and we have to ask several people until we meet somebody who directs us there. The centre is a memorial to those German officers who plotted against Hitler and who were executed in the courtyard, and also to other resistance groups who fought against nationalism. It's a light, bright place, with photographs and explanations, and a really fascinating look at the different factions who tried to overthrow Hitler and the Nazis. There's a virtual tour online here:

https://www.gdw-berlin.de/en/offers/overview/exhibition-tour/

We had no preconceived ideas of what to expect of Berlin and its citizens, and any expectations we may have had are far exceeded by the wide streets, the cheerful atmosphere and buzz, the ease of travel, the number of places of interest and most of all by the friendliness of the people.

Everybody we talk to is helpful. I smile at them, flap my map and say '*Guten tag* (learned a new word!). *Bitte?*' and point to where we want to go. Many of them speak perfect English, and even those who don't go to great trouble explaining how to reach our destination.

My grandparents would not hear the word 'Germany' spoken. It was forbidden. My father would not forgive me for working for a German. Memories of WWll were still too raw for them, but we are constantly asking ourselves: 'How did our countries ever end up at war with each other?'

With our travel ticket, we can hop on and off wherever we wish, and spend one afternoon catching buses and getting off anywhere that looks interesting.

Our wanderings lead us to Rosenthaler Strasse, where we stop in a little Vietnamese restaurant for lunch. We each choose a banh mi – a large baguette crammed with an unfeasibly enormous quantity of vegetables and tofu. It's cheap and tasty, and the most unwieldy food I've ever had, with the filling spilling out from both ends and the two sides. I feel as if I won't need another meal for a week, and I also feel as if I need a bath by the time we've finished.

We set out to walk off this mammoth meal but have only gone a few yards when we see an intriguing sign: Woop Woop Ice Cream. So we venture in to find out more. Five minutes later, we're sitting outside on the pavement eating Woop Woop ice creams. They are custom made to order, from a mouth-watering selection of flavours which are added to the basic ice cream mix, then put into a glass cabinet and processed with liquid nitrogen to create a silky ice cream in 30 seconds. I have popcorn and salted caramel, Terry chocolate chip cookie.

We're planning to take a long leisurely walk to digest all this food, but just then a tram stops nearby, so we hop on and see where it takes us. We get off at Friedrichstrasse Station and take a cruise up and down the river Spree, giving views of many of Berlin's iconic buildings and parks. We have taken a risk coming here in October, but have been blessed with exceptionally warm and dry weather.

When the cruise ends, it's early evening. We find a bar beside the river and sit looking at the station, thinking of its history during the Cold War.

Sitting here on a balmy evening, drinking a fine German beer and listening to the laughter of people all around us, it's impossible to imagine life here thirty years ago, just before the wall came down. With my poor knowledge of geography, I confess before we came I had no idea that the city of Berlin was geographically in East Germany when Germany was partitioned after the Second World War.

I knew of course that there was an East Berlin and a West Berlin, but hadn't appreciated that the whole city was actually enclosed in East Germany. The Berlin wall didn't only divide the city in half, it entirely encircled west Berlin, making it an Allied enclave within a Communist country.

I only now begin to understand the significance of Berlin in all those spy films, why the Soviets built the wall to stop people escaping communism and reaching the Western sector of the city which was controlled by the Western allies.

During the Cold War, West Germans could travel to East Berlin relatively freely to visit family. For people wanting to leave East Germany, it was far more difficult unless they were State officials or essential workers. Even those who were permitted to travel had to navigate a costly sea of bureaucracy, paperwork and interviews, leaving behind their identity papers to prevent them applying for West German citizenship. Families were unable to travel together, so relatives were effectively hostages, ensuring that visitors returned or had to leave their loved ones behind.

At that time, Friedrichstrasse Station was geographically in Eastern Berlin – it was the main border crossing between east and west sectors, and a 'gap' in the wall. The station was partitioned so that East and West travellers were divided from each other, and it was where friends and families said farewells when returning to their own sector, hence part of the station was known as the Palace of Tears.

With our handy map of all the railway stations, it's easy to find our way back to our accommodation. It's just a thirty-minute train ride.

After two days, we are completely hooked on Berlin. Despite its sinister history, there is nothing grim about the atmosphere; it is wonderfully vibrant and full of life. It is impossible to see this bright, friendly city as the setting for so much horror during the last war and the Cold War. There are many museums and monuments recalling the dark days, but there is nothing dark about the city. The streets are wide, there are beautiful parks and so much to see and do. The Berliners go out of their way to be helpful.

We spend a morning at the Berlin Zoo. We don't entirely agree with them, but for some species their survival depends on the conservation work and breeding programmes carried out by zoos. We go primarily to see the giant pandas, which we do, briefly, as they lumber slowly into view for three paces, then turn head over heels and lie down to take a rest in their magnificent enclosure.

The zoo is well laid out and well signed; all the animals seem healthy, content and well cared for. The exception is the elephants which are confined in far too small an enclosure.

For entertainment value, the sea lions win. Their exuberance is a joy to watch, as they race and chase each other in their spacious pool and clearly enjoying showing off to their audience. There's a great aquarium too.

In the afternoon, we visit the Topography of Terror, a modern museum on the site of the old Gestapo headquarters, giving an interesting and chilling look into life under Nazi rule. The topic is grim but the exhibition is well laid out and a fascinating, sobering insight into inhumanity and courage.

One of the highlights of our stay is a meal at a Michelin-starred vegetarian restaurant with the peculiar name of Cookies Cream. Adina has managed to book a table for us, which is a stroke of good fortune as people generally need to book months ahead.

Dining there is more than just having a meal; it's an adventure finding the place and if I hadn't been forewarned, we may never have reached it. Even with the directions written down, we almost miss it.

From the bright main Behrenstrasse road, we turn off next to the Komische Oper into a dingy alley lined with dustbins and empty pallets. It looks just like the kind of place you might expect to be mugged. We continue until we reach a bicycle lock-up and some storage sheds, at which point we discuss turning back. However, a little further on, there is a chandelier hanging in the alley, beside some concrete steps decorated with a decaying sofa and a rusty freezer.

If I had not read the reviews before coming here, I would have thought that this was some kind of Berlin joke. At the top of the steps is a plain brown door, and beside it a simple board announcing that we have arrived at Cookies Cream. So far it has been a rather creepy experience, like one of those old black and white Cold War films.

We buzz the door, which opens into a plush, cosy bar. Here we sip a cocktail until our waiter comes to take us to our table, up a metal staircase, rather like a fire escape, into the open-plan dining area. It's spacious and brightly lit, situated in an old industrial workshop with a concrete floor, bare brick walls and exposed cables and pipes in the ceiling. The tables, cutlery and crockery are shining and spotless. The waiters and waitresses are helpful, discreet, friendly and efficient, and explain each dish thoroughly.

We start with the vegetarian caviar with avocado, and the quail's egg in brioche. Both are exquisite – the quail's egg I could eat every day of my life and never tire of it. I've no idea how they make the vegetarian caviar, but it tastes like the real thing.

For main course, we both opt for the Parmesan dumplings with truffle sauce, two of our favourite flavours and a marriage made in heaven. We follow up with cornflake ice-cream and the hazelnut panna cotta, both light in texture and subtle in flavour, a perfect end to our meal.

With a bottle of wine between us, and a complimentary Fra Angelico and lime cocktail, the bill for our three courses come to just under 120 Euros. It's more than we would generally spend for a meal, but worth every cent. The food is SO good; celebs and dedicated carnivores regularly eat here, while its quirky location and decor make it a unique experience.

We've only been here three days, but we have already seen and done so much that it feels longer, and we could not be luckier with the weather which blesses us with warm sunshine every day. It's ideal for a guided tour to get to know more about the city.

Our tour guide is an Israeli who evidently loves the city and its history. Over the next three hours, we visit Bebelplatz, where the Nazis burned 20,000 books. The event is commemorated by a glass plate in the cobbled courtyard. Looking down into it, you see tall rows of empty book shelves, and a heap of ash. We see the place where President Kennedy made his famous speech, where he either said that he was a Berliner, or a jam doughnut, according to which version you believe. It seems to be all about the inclusion of the German word 'ein'.

Next, we pass the Fernsehturm television tower which was built by East Germany and intended to demonstrate Communism's superiority. It soars up into the sky and is visible from just about everywhere in the city. On a fine day from the viewing platform at the top, viewers can see for more than thirty miles. At 1,200 ft. it is 150 ft. taller than the Eiffel Tower. If you stand at the base and look up at the top, it gives you a crick in the neck.

We walk on to the Brandenburg Gate (the elephant-trunked man on a bicycle is no longer there) and the nearby memorial to the murdered Jews of Europe. This is a square filled with a collection of gigantic stone rectangles of varying heights, set out like a labyrinth, and disconcertingly, it slopes slightly, leaving you feeling rather discombobulated.

Our guide is full of interesting facts, and patient answering our questions. It's a three hour walk, and we stop for a short refreshment break at Checkpoint Charlie which is next door to a McDonalds.

This iconic, historic landmark is so awful I can hardly describe it. It is a tacky hut surrounded with sandbags, manned by actors wearing ill-fitting, faux-Russian uniforms and big furry hats, charging people to have their photos taken with them. We are so disappointed. Everywhere else we have visited and seen has been dignified and tasteful, so why this abomination is there I cannot imagine.

Anyway, off we go again, and our disappointment is dispelled when we reach a six-storey building on Niederkirchnerstrasse. We listen to a wonderful tale of daring and courage about an East German engineer who planned to escape over the wall with his wife and child, using a zip wire. The story goes that on a visit to the Government building he took his wife and son with him, and hid them in a lavatory, hanging an 'Out of order' sign on the door. Late at night, they climbed onto the roof, from where he hurled a rope attached to a hammer over the wall to friends waiting on the other side. They attached a metal cable to the rope so he could haul it onto the roof. Using a contraption made from a bicycle wheel, the whole family zip wired over the wall to safety. I can't imagine how much bravery that took for all of them, and I'm fairly certain I would have fallen off.

We go to inspect a remaining part of the wall, which is smothered in graffiti, and are surprised by how thin it is; it looks as if a good push could knock it down. On the other side, there had been a heavily-guarded and booby-trapped corridor of 160 yards and then a second wall to climb before reaching safety.

I mentioned earlier my very sketchy understanding of exactly what and where the Berlin wall was, and its significance. It has all fallen into place now and I can see the immense challenges involved in escaping to the West. I am always fascinated by the history of the places we visit. Berlin supplies that in abundance.

Our tour leads us to the splendid Gendarmenmarkt square and the imposing Konzerthaus, home of the Berlin orchestra. The concert house is flanked by two almost identical baroque churches, the French Church and the German Church. The Protestant French Church was built for the benefit of the many Huguenots who made their home in Berlin when they fled religious persecution in France. The German Church was Lutheran. I always believed they were the same thing, but apparently not if they needed separate churches.

We've lost a few of our group. At Checkpoint Charlie, they went to eat at McDonald's and although we waited for them for a long time, they never reappeared.

Our tour ends on a small nondescript patch of ground sandwiched between an apartment building and a car park. The guide invites us to look around to see if we can spot anything unusual or interesting in our surroundings, but try as we might there is nothing out of the ordinary to be seen.

'You may wonder why I chose to end our walk here,' he says.

Yes, we all agree. It isn't very exciting, rather an anticlimax.

'There is nothing to see,' he continues, 'because it all lies beneath our feet. We are standing over Hitler's bunker, which was demolished and flooded with concrete to prevent anybody accessing it in future.'

The site, incidentally, is in what was previously East Berlin.

There is just a small notice board in the adjoining car park mentioning the bunker, otherwise you would not know it was there. Berlin wants no monument to the monster responsible for so many millions of deaths in

WWll.

This has been such an interesting tour, and really given me such a clear picture of what Berlin means.

I learned a new word today: *rathaus*. I've noticed there are a lot of them about. It means 'town hall'.

Next day, we take a train to the heavenly lake at Schlachtensee, a two-minute train ride from Mexikoplatz station. The lake is surrounded by forest, and despite the glowing autumnal colours of the trees, it's still so warm there are many people bathing in the lake. A lady comes and sets down her belongings not far from where we are sitting. She undresses and carefully folds her clothes, then walks nakedly into the water and swims out sedately, returning after ten minutes to dry herself and dress again.

It's such a beautiful area that I decide to stroll around the lake, telling Terry I'll be back in forty minutes. From where we are, the geography doesn't show quite how far it is; there's a bump sticking out that looks like the edge of the lake, but hides the fact that there's a whole lot more lake on the other side. When I discover that, I stop strolling and begin a kind of hobbling jog because it's twice as far as I had thought, the path is uneven in places and you have to climb over some fallen trees. It takes almost two hours and Terry has set off to look for me.

From Zehlendorf, we take another short train ride to the pretty town of Potsdam. I am keen to visit Sanssouci, the little château built by Prussian king Frederik the Great as a place to entertain his family and close friends during the summer. It takes us longer than expected to walk there from the station, and it's a shame that by the time I have managed to climb up the 130 steps with my aching legs, the ticket machine has shut down and we can't go inside.

Still, the gardens are beautiful, as is the weather, so we wander around the town and go for a coffee. When we come back to Berlin, as we definitely will, we'll devote a whole day to exploring Potsdam. My heart misses a beat when I see, sitting quietly beside its owner, the ghost of Talisman, our Hungarian Vizsla who died not long ago. The likeness is so exact that I call 'Tally!' and the dog turns its head to look at me. I'm looking into Tally's eyes and it's a truly unnerving experience.

Sunday is our final full day in Berlin, and we go to visit the flea market at Boxhagener Platz. It's the furthest east we've been during our stay, and has a very different vibe from sophisticated central Berlin. The area here is arty, boho, busy, and the Communist era buildings are brought to colourful life with murals and graffiti. The air is fragrant with the aromas of roasting coffee and spices, the pavement cafés crowded with young families. We manage to squeeze into a small restaurant and treat ourselves to a Russian hot chocolate (20% vodka!) and a brunch of poached eggs in Hollandaise sauce with broccoli, grilled red peppers and sweet potato fries, all served on a sheet of brown paper.

Then we go bargain hunting at the flea market where we are offered a violin, old Russian cameras, fur coats, blue movies, hats, foods and flowers, religious icons, furniture and a beautiful old oriental rug that I would have loved if we had room in our luggage for it. There are sunglasses and Doc Martens, military greatcoats, shopping baskets, games and ornaments. Terry buys an illustrated book of beetles (in German) and I find a unique, slightly wonky model giraffe made by a local artist, unusual because instead of being giraffe patterned, it has been decoupaged with mixed wildlife designs. He wants more for it than I'm prepared to pay, considering it has a small break, but a few minutes of friendly haggling leads to a result that satisfies both of us.

The next morning on the train taking us to the airport, a long-haired man in our carriage stands and plays a violin, a haunting tune that highlights my sadness at leaving this magical city. In the short time we have been here, it has become so familiar. Although we have only touched the surface, we feel very at home here.

I'm concerned for my giraffe. It has a very long slender bendy neck and very long slender bendy legs, and I think it could easily break if it was handled roughly. I am carrying it wrapped in tissue in a shopping bag.

As we pass through the security check at the airport, I lay it very carefully into a plastic tray. As the security officer lifts the bag, I say: '*Das ist sehr delikat.*'

I have no idea at all where those words came from, or even if they are correct, they just seemed to spring from my mouth of their own accord. She smiles and picks up the giraffe, and nods. '*Ist schön*' she replies, handing it back. Great heavens, I've had a conversation in German.

37. Arizona

Through a strange series of events, we find ourselves in Arizona for several weeks, staying in the town of Sierra Vista.

It's our second visit to America, and quite different from our holiday on Captiva Island in Florida. Everything there was flat and luxuriant, surrounded by the warm waters of the Bay of Mexico, inhabited by the biggest spiders I've ever seen and a large alligator living in the ornamental lake in the complex where we stayed.

Here in Arizona, it's predominantly dust-coloured and mountainous and surrounded by scratchy bushes, with frequent monumental lightning storms that light up the skies at night. There are scorpions, rattlesnakes and a variety of poisonous spiders.

The first thing that strikes me here is the size of food portions. There are 32 oz. burgers, and ice-cream served in half-gallon buckets. There are restaurants serving self-help breakfast buffets that include cheese sauce, raspberry jelly, muffins, bacon, fried chicken and muesli. We see people mixing all these things together on the same plate and going back for more.

The second thing that strikes me is the friendliness and hospitality of the people we meet. They just cannot do enough for us.

We have the full Arizona treatment. Visits to cactus museums, trips to the Saguaro National Park to see the giant cacti, visits to a hummingbird place where the birds sit on us and on our cameras, and to the Old Tucson Studios where many Westerns had been filmed. (Sadly, this would be largely burned down soon after our visit).

Our hosts insist that we must buy a genuine pair of beautiful, tooled-leather cowboy boots, and take us to a store that has probably the largest selection of the boots in the world. That is when I learn that cowboys must have the most slender, flexible feet and ankles known to mankind, as no matter how we all struggle, I am unable to get my normal-sized feet and ankles around the bend in the boots. We push and pull and tug and twist. The only boots which I can fit my feet into are four sizes too large, with several inches of empty space in the pointy toes. They are high enough to cut into the back of my knees, but we buy them anyway as it seems the only way to leave the store.

We get used to seeing people wearing guns. We feed bats at night, tossing up morsels of meat into the sky and watching them swoop down.

In the historic, arty little town of Bisbee, we learn that the customer is not always right. Our hosts take us to a restaurant where everything on the menu contains meat. Everything. The nearest we can find to suit us is eggs Benedict, which we order, asking for it to be served minus the bacon. It arrives, complete with bacon. We ask the waiter to change it, and it comes back again, with bacon. According to our waiter, the chef can't serve eggs Benedict without bacon, because then it isn't eggs Benedict. We eventually negotiate to have a toasted muffin topped with poached egg and hollandaise sauce, which the waiter pointedly refers to as 'your order, which is *not* eggs Benedict'.

Next day, we visit Dragoon Springs, site of what was once a station for the stagecoaches and scenes of battles with Cochise Indians, and again during the American Civil War. All that remains is a tumble of stones, but surrounded by hills and the dry, scrubby terrain, it doesn't require much effort to imagine galloping horses, war whoops, shots and battle cries. Small cairns of stones mark the final resting places of those people who still lie in Dragoon Springs.

The vastness of the country – this is the heart of the Sonora desert – and the blue skies remind me of Africa. The road signs peppered with bullet holes remind me of the Wild West. I'm invited to ride out on a Western saddle, and feel slightly ridiculous wearing sandals - the only footwear I have with me - but my mount isn't bothered and I enjoy the easy relaxed style and the novelty of neck reining.

At lunch, I am surprised when, as we sit down, the head of the household says: 'And now let us pray for what we will receive'. I start to giggle because I think they are joking, but it turns out that they are all deeply religious Seventh Day Adventists. Oops.

Tomorrow, they say, we have a real treat in store, spending a day with them working on the ranch. I've no idea what that entails, I hope it's more horse riding.

It isn't. Sheree, my new cowgirl friend is very excited when she comes to pick us up next day.

'We just killed a cow for you,' she says with a huge smile.

We both look at her blankly.

'Why?' asks Terry.

'To give you a taste of some real good American beef steaks,' she replies.

It was only the day before yesterday when Sheree and her brother had taken us to Bisbee, and we had the altercation with the waiter over the fact that we don't eat meat. This fact had clearly not registered, or been forgotten.

It is excruciatingly embarrassing to have to say that we won't be able to eat the steaks, particularly as they have killed a whole cow on our behalf, but when I mention it she tells us not to worry, as we can eat something else. There are plenty of other people coming to the ranch.

We arrive at a small clearing among the shrubland, where riders are herding young calves into a wooden corral. 'Oh no,' Terry whispers, 'tell me they're not going to kill them?'

No, no killing. Instead, the calves are being branded and castrated. The noise is horrifying, the smell of burnt hair is awful, but it seems to these ranching folk that this is a merry event and something we will really enjoy. So we try to show enthusiasm as calves testicles are added to a wooden box to go on the barbecue with the remains of the cow that was killed for us.

At one end of the corral is a bull, and behind him a very young calf. As one of the men tries to lasso the calf, the bull stands himself in front of it.

'See that?' asks one of the ranchers. 'That old bull is saying the little fellow is too young today. We'll leave him until next time.'

When the branding is over, they start grilling the meat, and Sheree reminds them of our peculiar eating habits. We apologise profusely, but they are very understanding. Somebody has a sister who doesn't eat meat.

As there is nothing else on the menu, Sheree drives to her farmhouse and comes back with some bread which we eat politely.

Once the food is finished, we are going to play with guns, and I don't mind that. I used to do target shooting.

In the distance, we hear a gunshot. Five minutes later, one of the ranch hands rides up with a dead rattlesnake which he hangs from a tree and skins as we watch in fascinated horror.

When he says: 'We can't have you folks going hungry', we realise that this has been done specifically for us, because we don't eat meat, and presumably rattlesnake is not regarded as meat. There is no possibility that we can refuse in the face of such thoughtfulness.

Once the snake has been cut into slices, it's grilled and we are each given a hearty chunk, while a small group watches eagerly as we taste it.

'Mmm, very tasty,' says Terry.

'Yes, delicious,' I agree.

In fact, it is bony and rather oily in taste, but we both put on a show of eating it with gusto, while discreetly chucking as much as possible out into the bushes. It doesn't go unnoticed by the dogs who clear up the evidence.

We spend an hour playing with pistols, shooting at bushes and bottles, and so our day comes to an end, agreeing that we are not at all cut out for life on a ranch.

Sierra Vista is only a short drive from Tombstone, and we visit there several times. We are expecting a Disney-style theme park, but it's really interesting and there's nothing tacky about it. In fact, if the road wasn't hard surfaced and there was no street lighting, you could think it hadn't changed for over a hundred years. As fans of Western films and fiction, it is like stepping back in time, with wooden sidewalks, hitching rails, and bullet holes in the walls of the Birdcage Theatre where once gentlemen entertained young ladies in balcony booths. The hearse that had delivered the deceased to Boot Hill graveyard now stands there as an exhibit. Notices said to have been posted by Wyatt Earp show images of villainous 'Wanted' people, and signs down the main street point to where people were shot dead.

A colossal rose tree grows there, the largest in the world. It spreads over 9,000 feet, supported by a framework. The root was brought from Scotland, and somehow manages to thrive in this harsh desert environment.

One Saturday afternoon, we watch a slick re-enactment of the gunfight at the original OK Corral, convincingly played out by actors and acrobats, and then go for a meal and beer at Big Nose Kate's Saloon Bar.

There's a small band playing Country and Western.

When I was a little girl, I fell in love with a haunting song that became a huge hit worldwide, and I've loved it ever since. I ask Terry if he'll request the band to play it.

After half an hour, I've about given up hope. Suddenly the tune starts, and as it does every rancher/cowboy in the room rises to their feet and leads their wives onto the floor to dance. The men are all tall, lean, dressed in jeans, check shirts and cowboy boots, and their ladies are all short and wearing cotton frocks, looking like dolls as their menfolk twirl them around the room to the beautiful Tennessee Waltz, with the ladies' feet barely touching the ground. For those few magic minutes, it's as if we're taking part in a film – *Seven Brides for Seven Brothers*.

As I've mentioned, the thing I particularly love about travel is the history of the places we visit, the older the better. America's history is still young, but here in Tombstone today, it really feels as if we have travelled back in time.

On our last day, we are invited to go to Mexico for the afternoon. We cross the border at Nogales, and hit a bumpy, pot-holed road.

'Ya have to drive real slow here,' says our driver. 'No more than 20 miles an hour. If the Mexican cops catch you even one mile an hour over the limit, they'll bang you up in a cell.'

I watch the speed indicator carefully.

We reach some kind of yard and are left to sit in the car while our driver goes to talk to some people leaning against a shed. It's extremely hot in the car, so after five minutes, I get out and take a little walk.

There's a shout, a blood-curdling snarling noise, the rattling of a chain, and the biggest, angriest dog I have ever seen leaps at me from behind a container with its teeth bared.

An arm wraps itself around my waist and pulls me out of range.

'Señora, be careful. This dog will kill you.'

From the little we have seen and heard, Mexico seems to be quite a dangerous place.

I had hoped it would be possible to get to Pima, to visit the grave of the American grandfather I never met, but it's over 120 miles away from Sierra Vista, and we run out of time.

Sometimes we both feel the need for a small, simple meal, but it's elusive. Even small meals are vast for our appetites, and nowhere seems to serve fresh vegetables or salad as we know it or in quantities suitable for just one or two people. Back at Heathrow, we pull into a small supermarket on the way home and I buy a sliced white loaf, some butter and some fresh tomatoes. Never have tomato sandwiches tasted so sublime.

38. Londonderry

It's 1983, and there is a 'straight line' air race from London to Londonderry in Northern Ireland, commemorating Amelia Earhart's solo flight from America to Ireland in 1932.

The race starts from Leavesden airport, slightly northwest of London. It's during the time of the bombings by the IRA, and they have sent a warning that they will be targeting a major sporting event this weekend. All the aircraft are subjected to meticulous scrutiny ahead of the race. I flew with Terry on a 'straight line' race to Rotterdam, but on this occasion his friend is flying with him and I'm travelling with the committee in a twin-engined plane, to arrive in Londonderry ahead of the finish of the race.

When we land at the airfield in Londonderry, a brass band strikes up playing *Congratulations*. The local press is here too, and as we descend from the aircraft the crowd break out in a great cheer. Local ladies hand round trays with plastic cups filled to the brim with a choice of neat gin or Guinness, and mountains of chocolate éclairs. Even when we explain that we are not competitors, but the organisers, that does not diminish their enthusiasm or welcome.

Once the competitors have all arrived and been thoroughly welcomed, we are taken to our hotel in a coach. Passing through beautiful, lush green fields bordered by hedges, I think how sad that such a beautiful country is the setting for such a horrible war.

The Mayor of Londonderry is hosting a dinner for us at the town hall. A bus takes us from the hotel to the town hall, where the windows are boarded up, and we have to walk from the bus into the hall through a wire cage.

Dinner is rather reminiscent of boarding school. We sit on benches at long tables on which there are plates piled with slices of bread and butter. The mayor and local dignitaries are seated on the stage.

During the meal, somebody remarks that one by one, the men on the stage are slipping away out of sight. A rumour starts spreading that there has been an IRA attack. When one of the ladies on the stage stands up and begins singing *a capella* as if nothing is happening, it feels rather disconcerting.

However, all is well. The gentlemen are discovered in the men's lavatory with a small television, watching Irish boxer Barry McGuigan fighting.

The next morning, one of the pilots finds a note pushed beneath the door of his hotel room. It reads: 'Go home, English bastards.' However, as we have been met with nothing but warmth and kindness during our visit, we decide the note was a prank played by one of the pilots.

39. Luton

As unbelievable as it may seem today, when I was leaving school in the mid-1960s, we were given no career guidance. I was not aware that women could have any career other than nursing, teaching or secretarial work.

Now, looking back, if it had been possible, I would have liked to have been an engineer, but it wasn't an option. I chose to become a secretary as the lesser of three evils. It wouldn't take years to qualify before I could earn an income, which I had to do to support myself, and I wouldn't be clearing up sick and blood, or dealing with feral children like myself.

I suppose most jobs come with perks of one sort or another. My first job after leaving college was working at an auctioneer/estate agent. It was poorly paid, and although my official title was Secretary, I was a one-woman, odd-job, multi-machine working for six people, doing everything from arranging the flowers to valuing properties. Sometimes my head was spinning from the workload, but it was always interesting and I learned a lot. I especially learned to despise the forerunner of the photocopier, the filthy Gestetner machine on which I had to print the catalogues. A perk was the fatherly auctioneer who always asked me if there were any items I was interested in (it was always horse-related). If so they would pass under the hammer faster than the eye could see.

After that, I worked as a secretary at a brewery, where I was entitled to a crate of beer every week, something my father appreciated.

There were no perks for the four days I worked for IBM, but we did have a small earthquake which was exciting as the typewriters began sliding down the desks. That's where I learned that if you are caught in an earthquake, the safest place to stand is in a doorway. So far I haven't had to put it to the test, but it's useful to know.

Unfortunately, I was unable to get to grips with IBM's proportional spacing golf ball. It was a horrid thing, replacing the keys on a traditional typewriter with a rotating ball that travelled back and forwards along the carriage. That in itself wasn't a problem, but the proportional spacing was a nightmare, because each letter occupied a space adapted to its width. A 't' could take two, or possibly three spaces, and an 'm' or 'w' five or possibly six, so if you made an error and had to backspace and blank out the wrong letter and retype it, it was impossible to align the golf ball in the right place. At lunchtime on the fourth day, I was asked to leave.

I worked for a car concessionaire where I think there may have been some discount on a car purchase for employees, but as I couldn't afford a car it wasn't of any use.

Then I landed my dream job, working for a one-man business, a very much larger than life man who travelled overseas extensively. While he was absent, sometimes for many weeks, my only task was to check the morning mail and let him know if there was anything important. The rest of the time was my own to do with whatever I wished. Half my salary was paid in Liechtenstein. He could occasionally lose his temper, and he didn't mind if I lost mine. If we fell out, he would go out and return with some cream cakes or a present for my children. I loved every moment of the years I worked for him. I'd never have another job I loved so much.

Since then, I've worked in many places and done many things, including as a machinist in a factory and a cleaning lady. Some were quite awful but I viewed each one as an experience and tried to learn something new.

Nothing could equal the financial services industry when it came to rewards. It was brutally demanding on new recruits hoping to become millionaires working as Financial Consultants, which was a euphemism for life assurance salesmen. The majority of them would fail, but for those who didn't, life was a ball. No longer was it the man from the Pru on his bicycle, knocking on doors to collect the weekly 6d. premium. Those with sufficient stamina and determination to succeed were driving

BMWs and Porsches; high achievers were driving Rolls-Royces, wearing designer suits and expensive watches. There was a great deal of money to be made. Incentives included expensive meals, luxury holidays, and most coveted of all, gold badges studded with diamonds or rubies in recognition of their achievements.

My job as a branch administrator was to deal with all the paperwork, and in particular to spot any suspicious activity, of which there was always a certain amount. Some of those who weren't very good at selling could be ingenious and creative, submitting applications that would earn them a high commission if they could keep the application going for just a few weeks until the next pay day. If it subsequently cancelled, they were probably long gone. I knew instinctively when there was something suspicious about an application even if at first sight it seemed correct, and I thoroughly enjoyed the challenge of finding the subterfuge.

It was a fun job. Most of the senior executives were showmen who would have really liked to be pop stars more than life assurance managers. They hosted monthly motivational meetings where the top producers were hailed to thunderous cheering and clapping until our hands stung. I found it rewarding in many ways, working with dynamic people, and watching nervous beginners start to gain their confidence and develop. Another aspect I particularly enjoyed were the monthly dinners for the top producers in the branch. There was a generous budget which allowed us to take them to the best restaurants. It was my privilege and pleasure to choose the restaurants, and unfortunately, for many of the younger salesmen it was often an ordeal. They studied the menus with dismay, having no idea of what they meant. Their preference was for a curry or McDonald's and they were bewildered by ingredients they had never heard of.

Among some of the more memorable characters from those years was one of the street canvassers, an elderly tenacious Dutch lady who would follow prospective leads onto buses, if necessary, to obtain their names and phone numbers. Street canvassers were paid by the salesmen for every lead that produced a sale and Juliana was one of the best. She arrived in the office one day and an argument broke out with one of the salesmen. It became very noisy, and there were clients in the office. Terry intervened nicely and tried to calm her down. She lost her temper and flew at him, grabbing him by the shoulders and kicking him on the shins with her hard leather shoes, in a scene reminiscent of the fearsome Rosa Klebb in James Bond's *From Russia With Love*

For a short time, we had an office cleaner called Gwen. She was a sweet, timid lady who never removed her overcoat or her woolly hat and always wrung her hands when she talked to me. As she refused to declare her address, we paid her in cash. I had the impression that she had suffered a tragedy or trauma in her life, as she was very well spoken and genteel but seemed to live in a permanent state of fear.

I'd chat with her while she was cleaning, and one evening she told me that she also worked at the Royal College of Surgeons, where her job was to feed hard-boiled eggs to the cancers. I said that sounded like a very strange diet for sick people, but no, she replied, they weren't for people, they were for the cancers themselves. It's a secret, she explained. People believe that cancers are cells in the body, but actually they are small crab-like creatures that grow out of eggs in our body.

'We all have them, dear,' she said. 'They are harvested and kept in glass boxes and fed on hard-boiled eggs so they grow large enough for researchers to study and examine them.' She trusted me never to tell anybody.

I was naïve enough to believe her.

Her next story was equally horrifying.

She would not be able to work tomorrow, she said, as she had to go to the doctor because her nipples were falling off.

This was another secret, something they didn't tell anybody, but it happens to everyone. At a certain age, your nipples peel away and fall off. She had tried sticking them back with plaster after first applying talcum powder, but they continued to fall off and she was worried that she'd lose them. She hoped the doctor could advise her.

I was still naïve enough to believe that too.

We never saw her again. Probably just as well, as I was having nightmares.

There was a time when I kept noticing oily stains on the back of my skirts. I couldn't work out where they were coming from, and it was a long time later that one of the consultants explained. A new arrival who was not making any sales had decided that it was because I had put a spell on her, so she had seen a witch doctor and bought some oil to rub onto my office chair to reverse the spell. I don't think it worked as she never did make any sales.

The star of the show was an explosive, red-headed exhibitionist with a small mouse-like husband. You never knew what she was likely to say or do next, but it was always outrageous and entertaining, and I am indebted to her for two of the most surreal meals I can recall.

Her cooking was extraordinarily wonderful. It is the only time I have eaten a salad that was entirely composed of flowers. Marigolds, roses, nasturtiums and pansies arranged in colourful spirals, I've never seen a more beautiful dish.

I've never seen a more peculiar choice of artwork for a dining room, either. Each of the three walls were decorated with brightly coloured and detailed 3 ft. tall paintings of her lady garden, painted by herself, signed and boldly entitled 'My Vagina'. If you looked anywhere apart from your plate, you could not avoid seeing one of them.

We return her hospitality by inviting them to Sunday lunch. She is less than five feet tall, and extremely round and voluptuous. She startles us by suddenly leaping up and crashing to the floor in perfect splits, then inviting Terry to lie on top of her.

Her husband sits very quietly, smoking continually and stubbing out his cigarettes in the butter dish until dessert, when he stands up and recites Eliot's *Ash Wednesday* which, with due respect to Mr Eliot, is interminably long and which I find to be total gibberish.

The bouncy red-haired lady disappears at some point during her husband's monologue. We call her and search the garden in vain, finally finding her curled up in the shower tray of the downstairs bathroom, with the heels broken off her shoes. It takes all three of us to carry her out to their car.

We need more characters like those, more people who don't conform and fit into rigid templates, because they are the kind of people who are remembered, with all their quirks, and who make me smile when I think of them.

In return for the hard work, long hours and stress of the job, the rewards are generous. As well as all-expenses paid holidays abroad, we are used to staying in the best hotels and eating in the best restaurants, so when the invitations to the company's Christmas dinner invitations arrive, we look at them in astonishment.

It must be a joke. This year's dinner will be taking place at a modest hotel – in Luton.

No offence is intended to Luton, but it's mainly known for its airport, from where many of the budget airlines fly. There is no other reason for going to Luton, unless you are visiting friends or family, or on business.

Invitees are outraged. Some declare that they have no intention of travelling to Luton and will be declining the invitation. It's a sure sign the company must be in serious financial difficulty if this is the best they can do this year. People are already talking of jumping ship because the signs are that this one is sinking. Management say that all invitees are expected to attend the dinner; there may be repercussions if they don't.

None of us are looking forward to staying at a chain hotel in Luton and eating at the restaurant, but we drive there and change into our evening finery – which will be completely wasted on Luton.

The evening goes from bad to worse when we assemble in the bar for pre-dinner drinks. An apologetic and harassed Managing Director announces that the hotel's dining room has a problem with the heating and we'll have to wear coats over our clothes. We are a very disgruntled crowd, and somebody suggests that we call a taxi and try to find a decent restaurant in Luton, if there is such a thing, where at least we won't have to eat in our coats.

Wrapped in our outdoor clothes, we stand around waiting for dinner to be announced, but instead we learn that unfortunately there has been a malfunction in the kitchen. Alternative arrangements have been made for us to eat elsewhere. The whole evening has turned into a farce.

We are ushered onto a coach, puzzled, angry and disappointed. How is it possible we have been brought to this dismal place, accommodated in a third-rate hotel and are now on a coach not even knowing whether or not we'll have anything decent to eat?

Driving through the dark streets, we look out of the windows in the vain hope of seeing an inviting restaurant, but then we leave the city streets behind us and are driving through the empty countryside. We pass a sign to Woburn Abbey. The coach slows down and pulls up at the entrance. Our coats are taken and we are led into the splendiferous Sculpture Gallery, where a fittingly wonderful meal is served in the company of the beautiful Three Graces in their white marble, near naked glory.

Spoiled, as we have been over many years, by luxurious events, this is the one I remember most, not just because of the uniqueness of the location, but by the fact we had all been so well taken in.

40. Cruising the Canal

In autumn 1987, Terry is missing the water. We see an advertisement for a motorboat to hire for a weekend cruise up to Gloucester on the Thames and Severn canal, not far from where we live in Gloucestershire. From the photos it looks comfortable, with curtains and a proper bed.

The morning before we are due to pick it up at the marina, the owner of the boat phones to say there is a change of plan. For a reason we don't fully understand, he has moved the boat down the canal and moored it to the bank a couple of miles further from the marina. We need to collect it from there at a very specific time in the afternoon, the only time he can be there to hand it over to us.

Obediently, we arrive at the designated location and find the boat there. It's a pretty little thing, painted dark blue with a turquoise roof. The owner is in rather a hurry, so quickly shows Terry the engine and its workings before he dashes off, warning that we must leave the mooring no later than 10.00 am next morning.

The cabin does indeed have a proper bed, there are curtains and the sun is shining. A pair of swans are admiring each other and themselves in the calm canal waters, and people strolling along the footpath stop to chat. One of them tells us that our boat has just been evicted from the marina because the owner did not hold a licence to rent the boat out and had not paid the mooring fees.

We decide to motor a little way up the canal before nightfall. The engine is slightly reluctant and spits and hisses, but Terry beats it into submission. We motor slowly until we find a mooring beside a little bridge leading to a very *olde worlde* pub with a flagstoned floor. It's very cosy. We sit on an ancient wooden settle by a blazing log fire, drinking local cider and eating scampi and chips. Walking back to the boat, the night sky is very dark, and the air is soft and mild. After a hectic week commuting to work in and out of London, it's blissfully relaxing.

The boat's cabin has rather a strong smell of fuel, so we leave the hatch open and fall asleep. Some time later, we are awakened by the boat rocking wildly. Somebody is hammering on the roof and there is a loud whistling and wailing noise coming from outside, as if a screech of banshees are surrounding us. My heart is thudding loudly in my ears. We are in this lonely place, naked and defenceless, and it sounds as if we are under attack by a gang of crazed yokels, with nothing to use as a weapon. Terry fiddles around until he finds a torch and I scream at him to close the hatch so they can't get in, but then maybe no, what if they set the boat on fire?

It's rocking so violently that it's impossible to stand up without hanging on to the overhead locker, and feels as if it could overturn. Terry sticks his head through the hatch and shines the torch.

'There's nobody here,' he calls, 'but there's a hell of a storm out there. There are branches falling on the roof.'

He goes outside and secures the boat tightly against the bank. It is still bobbing up and down, and there's absolutely nothing we can do except get back into bed and try to sleep. The wind continues to howl and we can hear trees cracking and falling. As long as I have a comfortable bed, I can sleep through pretty much everything, which I do.

When I wake up, Terry is already up and about removing fallen debris and branches from the deck and roof. Although the worst of the storm has died down, the wind is still strong and creating waves on the canal which, as Terry remarks, is something you don't see very often. With the boat bouncing up and down, it's too dangerous to boil the kettle to make coffee, so we cast off. Terry forces the engine into life so we can go to find somewhere for breakfast.

Outside, it's a scene of complete devastation, fallen trees lying higgledy-piggledy on top of each other alongside the canal. The pathway is impassable, heaped with tangled branches. Phutting along the canal, we can see how the landscape has been changed overnight. There are only a few trees left standing; leaves, plastic bags, items of garden furniture and various detritus floats on the water and litters the banks.

It is eerily quiet. People are standing around staring at the carnage. We call out to a group who tell us that the whole country has been battered by hurricane force winds that the meteorological department had failed to forecast.

As we bob our way towards Gloucester docks, where we will turn around, the boat's engine dies completely, resisting Terry's attempts to restart it. It's just floating around on the waves and turns sideways onto the canal. Meanwhile, there is a scull fast approaching, and it is heading directly towards us. I've always thought that travelling at high speed without looking where you are going is extremely foolhardy, and no more so than this morning, when very shortly they will crash into us and either smash themselves or the boat to bits.

I stand and scream at the top of my lungs, which has no effect either on the engine nor the rowers. Giving up on the engine, Terry grabs a rope and leaps onto the bank. The grass is wet and he slips, smashing his shins onto the railway track embedded in it. He lies gasping for a few seconds. A man runs to help him, pulling him to his feet, stepping on his glasses and breaking them. Between them, they drag the boat out of the path of the scullers who astonishingly sweep past, entirely unaware that they have narrowly escaped death.

We have breakfast in a nearby hotel, persuade the boat back into life and return it to its illegal mooring, cutting short our cruise and wondering why our relaxing weekend coincided with one of the fiercest storms to hit the United Kingdom in the 20th century.

41. Cindy

My Facebook profile shows a photo of fourteen-year-old me with the grey pony that I loved with a searing passion that still burns despite all the years that have passed, and still brings tears, and a lump in my throat.

I remember the day in 1960 when I first see Cindy. My father had advertised in the local newspaper for a pony for me and received three replies. We have seen one pony, and as a horse-mad teenage girl I love every horse I see, but we have agreed to see all three before making a choice. Today, we are going to see the second.

It's a lengthy drive along the Mombasa road which is corrugated and rocky, thick with red dust during the dry season, a quagmire of incardine mud when the rains come. In a few years, when Kenya's President Jomo Kenyatta travels to his holiday home in Mombasa, this road will be surfaced for his comfort, but on this hot, dry day, the wheels of my father's Peugeot 403 leave billows of red grit in its wake as we bounce along. Despite the heat, the car windows are closed against the choking dust. The cool air blower makes a noise, blows air that is not cool and circulates the smell of the leather upholstery.

My stepmother sits in the front beside my father, holding their new young daughter in her arms. In the back, my bare legs beneath my shorts stick to the hot seat. The fifty-mile journey from our home to our destination in the dry, barren area of Kajiado takes nearly two hours, given the state of the road. It seems to take forever. Usually, I am car sick when travelling in the back. Today, I'm so tightly wound that I don't even notice. My jaw is clamped tight and my hands hard fists in my lap, my shoulders rigid so that I can barely climb out of the car when we arrive at a parched farm, bumping down a rutted track to a typical Kenyan settlers' farmhouse.

A smiling woman – her name is Mrs Darling – comes towards us, shakes hands and exchanges a few words with my father. She smiles at me, and we follow her to a small, bare paddock. My stepmother stays seated in the car with her child.

In the paddock, stands a flea-bitten grey pony dozing beneath a droopy tree, flicking lazily with her tail at a cloud of flies.

Mrs Darling calls. 'Cindy!'

The pony's head comes up. She whinnies gently and walks over to where we are standing. She smells deliciously of hot horse flesh.

I put out my hand and she snuffles it with her soft grey muzzle which looks and feels like velvet, then investigates my pocket where there is a packet of Polo mints.

A farm worker puts a saddle and bridle on her and holds her head while I ride her around the paddock, until I'm confident enough to go on my own. She's strong and lively. As I've only ever ridden riding school hacks, I'm not ready for her yet, but although she shakes her head and pulls and kicks up her heels, I can tell she's saying: 'I'm just having fun. I'll never hurt you.' She is talking to me.

My father knows nothing about horses and I know very little. Could this pony have any defects we don't know about? Dangerous habits, problems with her feet or back, broken wind? We are completely green.

'What do you think, Sue?' asks my father.

Whatever faults she might have, they don't matter to me. I have found the pony for which I have waited so, so long. My heart bursts, tears stream down my cheeks and my shoulders heave up and down as I try to stop myself breaking into a full-blown crying fit. I want to sit down and sob, because I am so damned happy and suddenly exhausted. I blurt out: 'I want her.'

My father writes a cheque for £60, money saved by my stepmother from the housekeeping. In two weeks, Cinderella will arrive by train at Nairobi with a groom, who will ride her to the local stables where she is going to live.

She finishes off the packet of Polo mints and lets me kiss her on her minty mouth. I breathe into her nostrils, and she breathes back into mine.

Two weeks is going to seem a lifetime. On the drive home, I sit silently staring out of the window, seeing nothing except a flea-bitten, grey Arab-Somali pony. I can smell her on my hands and clothes, and if I had my way, I wouldn't wash or change until she arrives.

We never do view the third pony for sale.

That is my most poignant memory. Bittersweet. It makes me smile, and it also makes me cry.

Susie Kelly
January 2021

Acknowledgements

A very special 'thank you' to all those readers who continue to buy and enjoy my books. Without you, it wouldn't happen.

As always my sincere thanks to my editor and friend, Stephanie for her support and encouragement and the many laughs we share.

Terry, thank you for the tea and toast that has kept me going, and for relieving me of so many domestic chores, leaving me free to write. You have done so voluntarily and without complaint, for which I am more than grateful.

Thank you Jenny Sohst for your help with the kamakis, Andrew Ives for your proof reading, and to David Lewis, cartoonist extraordinaire, for your brilliant cover artwork.

Susie,
February 2021

Dear Reader,

I do hope you have enjoyed this book. If so, could you do me a great favour by leaving a review on Amazon or Goodreads? Just a few words is plenty. I would really appreciate it as every review increases the visibility of the book so that more readers can find it.

If you'd like to find me on social media, my Twitter address is @SusieEnFrance; Instagram: @susiekellly; Facebook (where I am mostly to be found): @SusieKellyAuthor at Susie Kelly's Books Page.

If you'd like to read more, here follows a list of all my books with links to their Amazon pages. Some are occasionally on 99p offer and, now and then, even free for a short time. We can let you know when this happens via my (very infrequent!) mailing list. This is the link to join: http://eepurl.com/zyBFP (All email details securely managed at Mailchimp.com and never shared with third parties.)

Thank you so much.

Susie,
February 2021

More Susie Kelly Travel Books

In Foreign Fields – How Not To Move To Francer
The trials and tribulations of moving a family and many animals from the UK to a run-down smallholding in SW France.

I Wish I Could Say I Was Sorry
A US, UK and Australian Amazon Top 40 Ranking Bestseller
400+ 4/5* Reader Reviews on US Amazon
Each time it seems things cannot get any worse, they do as the popular travel author lifts the lid on her own, often shocking, behaviour in her quest to protect herself and those she loves. Rebellious, lonely and self-destructive, it is a small grey horse named Cinderella who saves Susie from herself and brings her the love she craves.

Safari Ants, Baggy Pants & Elephants: A Kenyan Odyssey
The long-awaited sequel to *I Wish I Could Say I Was Sorry*. More than 40 years after leaving Kenya, Susie unexpectedly finds herself returning for a safari organised by an old friend. With her husband Terry, Susie sets off for a holiday touring the game reserves, but what she finds far exceeds her expectations. This is the link to the on-line album and slide show of Susie's safari: http://bit.ly/2rhZF1k

Swallows & Robins: The Laughs & Tears Of A Holiday Home Owner
Finalist, The People's Book Prize 2016
'Laugh out loud funny. A must-read for anyone dreaming of the good life running gites in France.' *The Good Life France*

The Valley Of Heaven And Hell
Novice cyclist Susie wobbles on her bike for 500 miles through Paris and Versailles, the battlefields of World War 1, the Champagne region and more. She follows the path of Marie-Antoinette and Louis XVI as they flee from the French Revolution. A wonderful mixture travel, history, humour.

Travels With Tinkerbelle: 6,000 Miles Around France In A Mechanical Wreck
Join Susie, Terry and 2 huge dogs on a 6,000-mile journey around the perimeter of France.

Best Foot Forward: A 500-Mile Walk Through Hidden France
When Susie decides, at the age of 50+, on a whim, to trek alone across France from La Rochelle to Lake Geneva in Switzerland, she entrusts her French farmhouse full of assorted animals to a total stranger from San Antonio, Texas.

The Lazy Cook (1) Quick & Easy Meatless Meals
The first of Susie's delightful round-ups of her favourite quick, simple, easy recipes, sprinkled with anecdote and humour.

The Lazy Cook (2) Quick & Easy Sweet Treats
'I like a dessert to make me feel slightly guilty about eating it, but not enough to make me stop.'

All of the above titles are also available in paperback on Amazon and can be ordered from good bookshops worldwide

La Vie En Rose (Blackbird)
A pick from some of the best bits of the popular travel author's blog diaries reveal the minutiae of expat day to day life in rural France. A must-read for Susie Kelly fans and anybody thinking of, or dreaming of, moving to France. FREE *Kindle only*

Blackbird Digital Books
The #authorpower publishing company
Discovering outstanding authors
www.blackbird-books.com
@Blackbird_Bks

Blackbird